GET HER ON BOARD

Secrets to Sharing The Cruising Dream

Nick O'Kelly

Illustrations by David Olberding

PUBLISHED BY:

Top Down LLC

Get Her On Board - Secrets to Sharing The Cruising Dream
Copyright © 2010 by Nick O'Kelly
Cover design by David N. Olberding
Book design by David N. Olberding

Visit my websites:

www.nickokelly.com

www.getheronboard.com

ISBN 978-0-578-05729-3

For Megan

Contents

Final Thoughts

Preface

"Honey, you're not seeing the same numbers here that I am," I said as I pointed limply to my carefully prepared spreadsheet on the laptop between us in bed. Megan glared at me and turned back to her *O Magazine.* It was an hour after our normal bedtime.

"I am NOT going to buy another fucking boat," she said without lifting her eyes from the page. "You are really pissing me off, you know that? You conned me into it once. I'm not going again. Been there, done that," she said, raising her voice just one notch. Her annoyance was understandable; I'd brought up cruising, sailing, or boats at least once a week for more than three years. I got a similar reaction each time.

I couldn't really blame her stubbornness and she had every reason to be irritated with me. The first cruise hadn't lived up to my promises. After spending two and a half years and just over two hundred thousand dollars preparing a sturdy 50-foot cutter-rigged sailboat with every possible luxury and safety feature, things hadn't gone so well.

Four days into our planned five-year cruise and 600 miles south of San Diego, we were caught in full storm conditions. For over 24 hours, we were pounded by 60-knot winds and up to 35 foot breaking seas as we crossed a seamount bank 70 miles off the coast of Baja, Mexico. If it hadn't been for the destination beach wedding in Puerto Vallarta (where we expected 60 friends and family) two months later, Megan would have flown home from Cabo San Lucas and put an end to *The Dream* in the first week.

Somehow I managed to convince her that the freak storm was just incredibly bad luck. She agreed to stick it out for another six months of very safe and conservative sailing in the Sea of Cortez, but I had to forget about the South Pacific or sailing around the world.

A year later and at a loss of almost $100K, the boat was gone, and with it *The Dream*; *My Dream*.

Since then, not a day went by that I didn't daydream about those days on *Low Pressure*. We had met wonderful people, seen so many beautiful things, and experienced life in a way that just wasn't possible ashore. In spite of the trials and misadventures, we learned so much about ourselves and each other and came to see life in a fresh new way. Even if it hadn't been what we expected, we agreed that it had been the most important and transformative experience of our lives.

It made me sad that Megan was completely closed off to going again (maybe even more-so than the first time) and that I was mostly to blame.

"Just so you aren't confused, I am NEVER going cruising again," Megan said in a voice that meant: *you better not bring this up again*. With that, she tossed her magazine on the floor, rolled over, and turned off her reading light. Any time Megan was willing to disrespect Oprah, I knew she was not happy.

Six months later, Megan folded her latest *O Magazine* in her cubby, snuggled up on my side of the v-berth of our new (to us) cruising sailboat, *Either Way,* and kissed me on the cheek. It was the end of another satisfying day out cruising on our own boat, and we both couldn't be happier.

How in the Hell Did I Do It?

How did I *Get Her On Board*...again? I changed everything: from how I perceived my life to what I expected from cruising to how I saw our relationship. I did it by approaching *The Dream* and my wife in a whole new way.

This book is for you. I want you to go cruising and have a fantastic time *out there*. This book will show you how to move past the stumbling blocks, put together a plan and more importantly a <u>team</u> to get going today. I wrote this book because if I'd read it eight years ago, it would have saved me a tremendous amount of time, money, and frustration.

When I first caught the cruising bug, I devoured anything and everything about the subject that I could find. The local marine bookstore had shelves full of books detailing the methods of sailing and cruising, romance-of-the-sea stories of triumph and adventure, and cruising guides detailing everything from the best reef passes to international check-in procedures. There were how-to books on the basics of rigging, diesel mechanics, fiberglass repair, sail making, and innumerable non-fiction titles covering every aspect of life at sea from cleaning to provisioning to cooking underway.

We aren't going to talk much about those things in this book; there's no need to re-hash what has written about a thousand times. Instead, this book is about the most important equipment on a cruising boat: *The Dreamers*.

Don't get me wrong, the how-to and do's and don'ts are important, but the truth about living *The Dream* is that you'll really only end up learning by <u>doing</u>. You'll learn about the best routes and destinations from other cruisers you meet *out there*. You'll learn how to anchor by dragging a few times and refining your technique. You'll learn how to bleed the fuel lines by changing a filter or two. In time, you'll become as comfortable navigating new landfalls as you are at parking your car.

You'll make tons of little, inconsequential mistakes: you'll strip a few bolts and wake to an anchor alarm a few times. Shit will happen, and you'll deal with it. Most of this is not rocket science, and you'll be competent and confident in a few months.

There is an entirely different class of mistakes; what I will call *critical* mistakes that will either derail your sailing dream before it gets started, or put a premature end to the cruise. These are the game-ending and dream-ending mistakes that are very difficult to recover from. I made many of these critical mistakes before and during our first cruise. Later I found that I wasn't alone and my story is not unique.

In ports all over the world you'll find fantastic deals on dreams run hard onto the proverbial rocks when their captains made these critical errors. This is a classified advertisement taken directly out of a popular sailing magazine:

> **For sale: Hylas 44, 1989. Low hrs.**
> **Exclnt Cond. SSB, wtrmkr, wndvne,**
> **Lfrft, RIB/15hp, new sails, dodger.**
> **Scrfc. $105,000. Lying Panama.**

If this boat was outfitted in the last three or four years and not holed in a hurricane, she is likely worth much, much more than what they are asking. This boat is not a one-in-amillion great deal; you'll find similar ads for boats in Puerto Vallarta, Ft. Lauderdale, Trinidad, Auckland, and maybe even one or two in a marina near your homeport.

The owner or broker will tell you that they are selling because of, "a change of plans," "unexpected illness," or, "it was just time to swallow the anchor," but when a boat is sacrificed like this, the situation is rarely as clean and dignified as that. These are messy situations; these boats are abandoned. Go take a look at her and you'll see other abandoned dreams berthed all around. These other owners just haven't accepted the reality quite yet. They pay the rent until the last hope of *going* is gone, and then they'll sell too.

It's sad. These boats represent years and years of sacrifice and saving and planning and hoping and preparing. Smart, intelligent people own them: successful businessmen, lawyers, inventors, engineers, doctors, craftsmen, contractors, and the like. A lot of these men waited their entire working lives for this single experience: to take to the sea on their own boat. Why do these dreams end up for sale at the end of a sun-bleached dock?

The same questions could be asked about most of the boats in your local marina. Some surveys indicate that most boats (up to 90%) leave their slips less than six times per year. ARE YOU KIDDING ME? Why do smart people purchase boats capable of (and with dreams of) sailing long distances but rarely if ever take them out of the slip for even a circuit of their local waters?

It's What's Under the Hood that Counts

My favorite analogy comes from cycling: it's the rider that makes the bike go fast. Here in Marin County (just north of the Golden Gate Bridge in the San Francisco Bay Area), we have some of the most incredible and scenic cycling terrain in the country. On any given weekend, you'll see hundreds of spandex-clad riders on beautiful 15 lb. carbon-fiber wondermachines with all manner of heart rate monitor and touch-screen navigation on their handlebars. Many of these bikes cost upwards of $7,000.

Overweight riders top a good percentage of these expensive bikes. Good for them to go outside and get some exercise, but spending an extra six thousand dollars to save four pounds of bike doesn't make a lot of sense when they would be much faster up the hills if they lost twenty pounds of body fat. And no matter how light their bike, they will never be able to go very far or very fast unless they get in shape.

On a cruising boat, it's not the radar, the mainsail, the watermaker, or even the engine that makes the boat go. It's you; it's *The Dreamers and The Dream*, not the equipment that makes the difference. If *The Dreamers* and *The Dream* aren't strong, the boat doesn't go far if at all. You can't buy *The Dream* from a yacht broker or at West Marine, and this is where many of us (me included) go wrong.

Let me not throw stones from my glass house! I am the first to admit that I have fallen asleep with an open West Marine catalogue on my chest many times. The proper windlass, the most elaborate electronic navigation, the oversized alternator, the scuba compressor, a fourth anchor, the asymmetrical spinnaker, etc., who among us doesn't like to talk about boat gear? Boat guys are gear-heads. But to focus on the boat and equipment at the expense of paying attention to what is really making this dream happen is a huge mistake that so many of us men make.

To go cruising and have a successful cruise, it is imperative that you understand that you and your wife or fiancé or girlfriend or partner or whatever you want to call her; you two are the engine that drives *The Dream* of sailing away from it all for a life of freedom, adventure and discovery.

Cruising is a Couple's Sport

That's right, I said you <u>two</u>. I believe that cruising is a couple's sport. I know I am going to catch some resistance here, but my opinion reflects the reality of the cruising lifestyle and those who are actually *out there* actively cruising. The fact is that the majority of cruising crews are a man and a woman of intimate acquaintance. This book is about making sure that the engine of *The Cruising Dream*: the <u>two of you in a loving relationship</u>, are in ship shape and ready for the challenge and the wonder you'll experience *out there*.

Solo sailors

I understand solo sailboat racing: a single person testing themselves and their boat in extreme endurance-I get it. Solo cruising? - I don't get it. In fact I am going to ignore the idea of solo cruising because the reality is that you'll find very, very few long-distance cruising boats *out there* with a full-time solo sailor aboard. The majority of, "solo," sailors that you do meet while out cruising fall into one of three categories:

1. Not really cruising, but more living aboard alone in a foreign port. Many were once part of a cruising couple.

2. Not really solo. Many solo sailors find that they have to take on crew for most legs of their journey for emotional, physical, or insurance reasons.

3. Waiting in port for their wife or girlfriend to rejoin the boat.

The real-deal solo sailors do exist of course; there are solo men and women out cruising by themselves, but they really are very few and very far between. They are unique people and they have rare abilities and traits; I have tremendous respect for them. However, I am not going to make apologies here: in my opinion, cruising is like sex or badminton; it is just one of those activities that are better when shared with someone else.

A quick note to those other exceptions

Yes, I know that gay couples cruise. Yes, I know that there are families with children that cruise. Yes, I know that there are female skippers that take their landlubber husbands out on the water or even captain the boat on extended cruises. I acknowledge all of you. You may find some useful advice in this book, but let me be clear: this book was written for the man with *The Cruising Dream* and a wife or fiancé, girlfriend or partner ("wife" from now on) who is new to sailing and cruising, and possibly/probably resistant to or hesitant about the idea whether she will admit it or not.

A Disclaimer

Throughout this book, you will find that I have used a broad brush and oversimplified both sexes where a much more nuanced assessment was possible. I have also used extreme examples, overstatement, and humor to make points. In writing the book, I found generalizations and stereotypes unavoidable. Where possible, I have cited research to back up anecdotal evidence.

In an attempt to pre-empt any criticism on my view of women, please let me say that **I believe that all people are individuals first, male and female second. I believe that women are capable of doing virtually anything that men can. All said, I think that women are superior to men in many, many ways.**

That being said, there are tremendous (and wonderful) differences between the sexes, and those differences are expressed in a myriad of ways. When it comes to the idea of sailing away from normal life on a little boat, the differences between men and women are VAST.

That the women in our lives will even occasionally indulge our male fantasies to captain our own boats to distant shores shows a level of commitment that most men would never, ever reach. How many men do you know that would follow the woman in their lives on a dream-quest of <u>her</u> making? Very few I think. How many men do you know who will even fly to Chicago with their wives to watch an Oprah Winfrey show taped? That's what I thought.

My intentions are pure: I want to see more boats leave their berths more often. I want to see more people realize *The Dream*. Getting Her On Board is critical to making *The Dream* a reality.

1.
Introduction

"Honey, let's take the boat out on Saturday," your wife suggests.

"You sure? It's supposed to be windy with a few showers."

"No biggie; I love being out in the elements. A little breeze means we can practice reefing!" She says enthusiastically.

"Wow, this will be the fifth week in a row," you say, "we're putting plenty of hours on the engine; I'm going to have to change the oil before we go."

"I can help you do that; no problem," she smiles, "in fact, I'd really like to learn how so that I can do it myself sometime."

"You're the best," you say, and kiss her on the cheek.

She goes on, "I was looking at some charts of the ICW and the Bahamas last night, and I was thinking how nice it would be to spend all of our vacation this year aboard the boat. You know, take a little trip and get a taste for what full-time cruising will be like in a few years. We could head to The Florida Keys again though if you'd like."

"What a great idea," you say, "but we'll have to do some upgrading for an offshore trip…"

She interrupts excitedly, "I've already made up some lists. I was thinking we should get a watermaker installed, and maybe a cruising spinnaker. We should probably buy a life raft and EPIRB too. I've got some savings stashed away for a rainy day; we could use that."

"A spinnaker, eh. I don't have any experience with those…"

"That's OK, I'm planning on taking some advanced sailing classes this spring," she goes on, "I'll learn the chute, and teach you how. That would be kind of fun. You know, the first mate teaching the captain…"

"Fantastic!" With a big warm bear hug you say, "honey, I love you so much."

Does this resemble a typical discussion with your wife? If it does, you can put this book down right now; there is nothing in here for you.

Can you imagine if this scene were anywhere close to your own reality? What if your wife were as enthusiastic, ambitious, and excited about sailing and cruising as you are? What would it be like if she participated with 100% effort? What would it be like if she was 100% supportive of *the cruising dream*? What *if your dream* was *her dream*?

Unfortunately for most of us men with the cruising bug, our wives bear no resemblance to the fictional character above.

The Dream

For us dreamers, *The Dream* is in-born; it's a part of who we are. We are filled with wanderlust, and the image of captaining our own boat across the ocean to beautiful and exotic landfalls is deeply ingrained. Your dream may vary, but it probably goes something like this:

Gliding just off the white sand beach through crystal-clear blue water in perfect 80 degree weather, your boat slices through very light chop with a steady breeze on the port quarter. Dolphins have been playing in the bow wake for the last hour. You're on your way to a protected anchorage where you can see the anchor easily in 30 feet of water.

Swinging gently on the hook, fish seek shelter beneath the boat while sea birds circle at a distance, occasionally diving on an unsuspecting target a few boat-lengths away. Your favorite music is playing on the stereo and the boat rocks gently with a relaxing rhythm. You've got a cool drink in your hand and all the time in the world.

This fantasy and others like it have launched a thousand cruising dreams, sold thousands of boats, and millions of books, magazines, and DVDs. *The Dream* is big business.

It's not a lie; *The Dream* is a reality: swimming with whales, befriending local islanders, trading pearls, dolphins dancing off the bow, tons of free time to do whatever you want; these are the experiences waiting for you *out there* right now. Yes, that is the reality of cruising. Yes, it really is that good. Yes, it really is within your reach. Yes, it really is worth all of the sacrifice necessary to do it. Yes, if you are thinking about it, you really should do it.

This dream of yours is not something that will go away with time. There is only one way to satisfy the hunger. You really must go.

Without Her, You're Not Going Anywhere

Before you do anything to make this dream a reality, know this: you are going nowhere without *her*; and I don't mean the boat. I am talking about your wife, the love of your life, fiancé, partner, girlfriend, or whatever you want to call that special woman in your life (from now on, by the way, we are just going to call her your, "wife"). I'll say it again for emphasis: unless she's on board with *The Dream*, you are not going to go.

I can hear you resisting. You might be thinking: I'll get her into sailing by buying this nice boat at the boat show, and I can do most of the work anyway; she can just ride along. Why wouldn't she want an unlimited vacation with me at the helm? Or maybe you think you'll just go by yourself. You've got visions of Joshua Slocum dancing in your head, piloting the *Spray* around the world alone as he did more than a century ago. You are not alone in these fantasies, but this kind of thinking is the very reason that few dreams become a reality.

Denial isn't just a river...

Sure, there are single-handed sailors out cruising by themselves, but they are a very rare species, and an odd one at that (they will be the first to agree). The simple fact is that the vast majority of those who end up actually *out there* cruising in a small boat on a big ocean are couples.

Go to any anchorage in a foreign port and count the single-handers (the real single-handers). Sure, you'll find solo liveaboards who were cruising at some point with someone else, and those with or waiting for temporary crew, but you won't find more than one in fifty full-time single-handed active cruisers. Here's why:

1. **Cruising is a lot of work.** It isn't necessarily hard work, but it is a lot of work; probably more than you imagine. Dividing that work between two people means less time on work and more time having fun. That's what you're out there for, right?

2. **Safety.** Sailing alone requires compromises when it comes to safety. You simply cannot stand watch all the time when you are running the boat by yourself. You must sleep, and while you are doing that, there are risks. Most wannabie solo sailors never completely accept those risks, and hence never set sail. Most insurance companies won't underwrite a voyage unless there are two crewmembers on board.

3. **Loneliness.** Human beings are social animals. Even the most unsociable loner needs some human interaction after a couple of weeks. Those that go without sometimes suffer mental stress or health issues. Many solo sailors end up taking on crew after a couple solo passages just for the company.

4. **Boredom.** You'll hear cruising described as days of boredom punctuated by a few minutes of sheer terror. This is very true, however the terror is never as bad as you imagine it will be, while the boredom can be much worse than anything you have ever experienced. Having a close friend to play Yatzee with is invaluable.

5. **Personal growth.** Going cruising is a life-changing experience. Every cruiser who has been *out there* I know talks about how much they grew as a result of the cruise. Yes, the highs are very high and lows are very low. You will face countless challenges that test every facet of your personality and learn what you're made of. Having someone intimate with which to share this life-changing experience is invaluable.

6. **Enjoyment**. Let's face it, some things are just more fun with someone else. Sailing and cruising are activities that are better shared. A sunset is always more beautiful with someone else there to see it, and the same goes for a cold drink after snorkeling, fish tacos, etc.

You can try to pursue *The Cruising Dream* alone, but your chance for success is low. How low, you ask? There are no statistics available on what percentage of would-be solo sailors actually go cruising, but the fact that you find so few *out there* doing it compared with the number you meet on the dock (or cruising boats purchased) is evidence that the percentage is likely very, very small.

You'll meet plenty of hopeful and apparently solo owners who say they want take their boat to Mexico, the Caribbean, or the South Pacific, "someday," but you can tell they aren't really going anywhere. Maybe they aren't keeping up with maintenance; maybe they aren't physically up to the task; but for whatever reason they seldom leave the dock even for a day sail. For these dreamers, having *The Dream* means owning the boat, and nothing more. So they keep paying the slip fee and showing up for a burst of effort a couple times a month. But actually *going* cruising? Not going to happen. Ever.

If you're not sure that I speak the truth, why do we find most perfectly capable sailboats bobbing in their slips on even the most perfect summer afternoon?. Life is just too busy? Missed the incoming tide? Can't go out until the new genoa arrives? I don't buy it. I think that there's a much more important ingredient missing that keeps the boat in its slip.

She's not on board

Many of these solo gentlemen with their capable boats sitting at the dock have a woman in their lives, but for whatever reason, she's not on board. The reasons could be many:

- She doesn't like the boat.
- She doesn't enjoy sailing.
- She doesn't trust him as captain.
- She doesn't like how he treats her when they are out.
- She may not even like being around him when he's on his boat.

As far as she is concerned, the boat is *his* business, and she doesn't want any part of it. She doesn't like competing for his attention, and resents the fact that he is into this boating stuff at all. On board with *The Dream*? She isn't even on board with him having *The Dream*.

Yet she is the critical element that can make *The Dream* into *The Reality*. If she were on board, whether for a day sail or a five-year cruise, you bet he'd go.

We are going to get her on board

I'm not going to bullshit you, this won't be easy. You're going to have to change the way you look at yourself, your dream, and your wife. You'll have to learn how to approach her with the idea of sailing away, deal with her inevitable objections to the idea, and persevere coolly instead of getting frustrated. You may even need to buy a different boat or change the way you are accustomed to captaining your boat.

Making accommodations for your wife's health, welfare, comfort and happiness is only part of the equation; more importantly you must realign your values as a couple so that she can and will buy into *The Dream* itself. If you can't or aren't willing to do this, you will never get her on board. This alternative; a dream unfulfilled is a much greater burden in my opinion. Regret and resentment for not sailing away on your own boat is one of life's true tragedies.

It IS Worth It

Getting her on board and keeping her on board will be a challenge, but it will be worth it, 100%. Ask any experienced cruiser with a few thousand miles under their keel what cruising is *really* like. They may tell you a tall tale, or recount a favorite destination, or give you some piece of advice about equipment or gear. Ask them if it really is worth it; worth the sacrifice; worth the effort. They'll give you a pause and look at you deeply to see if you are serious, then they'll tell you that it is. Ask them whether you should go, and they'll tell you that if you really want to go, you shouldn't wait. They wish they had gone sooner.

The crossings, the landfalls, the things we've seen, the places we've visited, and the people we've met make me smile while writing this. Seeing the world from the deck of your own boat is a special experience, and one that I won't waste page space recreating poorly for you. Suffice it to say that the cruising life is everything that you've read about in those books by Slocum, Hill, The Pardeys, Leonard, Palley, Hiscock, Roth, and the others. If you need a little brain candy, check out any of those authors to wet your appetite.

Megan and I have now gone cruising twice, and as you learned in the preface, the first experience didn't meet the expectations we'd created from reading those books. I abandoned *The Dream* of that first cruise with a ton of regret. I take full responsibility for what went wrong and blame myself alone for making so many avoidable mistakes. I learned from those mistakes, and approached and executed the second cruise from a completely different perspective. The second trip left us both wanting more.

Both cruises deepened our relationship in ways that are difficult to explain. Megan and I have trusted each other so many times and shared so many experiences never possible in daily life ashore. As a result we enjoy a stronger, deeper bond than we could have otherwise. We can and will survive anything that life throws at us, on or off the water.

Cruising has been the most important and life-changing thing that we have done in our lives; separately or together. It couldn't have happened; in fact it wouldn't have happened if it weren't for my wife getting on board and staying on board.

If you are dedicated to the idea of sailing away for your own adventure, get ready to make room in your fantasy for your wife. She is the first and last piece of *The Dream* that you need to consider. Get her on board and *The Dream* will become a reality.

2.

Why Go Cruising?

I know a little bit about you: you love being on the water, you love the ocean, you love the wind in your hair, you love the taste of salt spray on your lips and the feel of the helm in your hands. A properly trimmed sail makes your heart go pitter-patter. On occasion, you may have tasted your boat's bilge water to see if it was fresh or salty. Wet diesel exhaust smells good to you. Your eyes are drawn to open horizons and you are drawn to the mystery of what's on the other side. Aside from those things brother, I don't know anything about why you want to sail a small boat on a big ocean. Do you? In this chapter we do some soul searching and clarify:

- ✓ Why you want to go cruising.
- ✓ What you hope to get out of the experience.
- ✓ The basic plan you have in mind.
- ✓ Obstacles standing in your way.

Your answers and reasoning here are critical to sharing your dream. You want to get your wife to see sailing away from, "normal life," as you see it. You want her to love what you love and want what you want. I guarantee that unless you've found that one in a thousand girl who was born with small-boat sailing and cruising on her list of life-goals, your wife does not see *The Dream* the same way you do. So, in order to steer her ship to where yours is moored, we have to know where your anchor lies.

Why Cruising?

You're practical, analytical, logical, and able to see things the way that they really are; you're a man after all. You aren't as emotional and, "unreasonable," as a woman, right? Good. So let's face the facts here and call a spade a spade, friend: the undeniable truth is that going cruising makes no logical sense whatsoever. Pretending that it does won't help you convince your wife to go with you.

With so many other modern options available to explore, adventure, relax, or just, "find yourself," on this planet, what is it about sailing and cruising that resonates with you?

Jamaica is nice

Consider a few alternatives. Do you want to live off the grid? A motor home is less maintenance and more comfortable. Is it travel that excites you? Trains, cars, and airplanes are faster and a lot less expensive. Want to live cheap? Backpacking and camping are less expensive alternatives. Want to challenge nature? Mountain and rock climbing will test you more physically. Want to sail in a beautiful location? Chartering is quick and convenient. Want to relax on a white sandy beach? Jamaica is nice.

If you are really infected with the cruising bug, I suspect that the answer to the question, "why go cruising?" is more complicated than white sand beaches and living independently. Maybe it's the romance of the sea and the aesthetic of it all? Perhaps, but I believe that your motivations run even deeper. How else can you explain the desire to do something as expensive, time consuming, challenging, and life-committing as cruising?

20

Cruising as art and expression

There is something special about this *cruising dream* of yours; something you just can't put your finger on. Cruising has an element of the intangible; there is something uniquely expressive and transformative about setting off on a trip under sail, and you feel it down deep. You know intuitively that sailing your own boat over a vast ocean to see new things, places, and people will somehow change you.

I propose that sailing is your art, and what you create is the voyage. The canvas is your life and those that you touch along the way.

There are no alternatives that compare. Pulling an RV into a trailer park is not art. Where is the personal expression in getting on a plane or hopping a bus? I don't see the same level of creation in living out of a backpack. Mountain and rock climbing do qualify as art in my book, but the experiences are not as long and all-encompassing as cruising in a small boat. Chartering is a great way to taste the cruising life, but it's a little like going to a concert compared to playing one. Jamaica is nice, but a white sand beach by itself is not creation, it's recreation.

None of the experiences above compare to that of full-time cruising on a small boat:

- Living away from the dock on your own boat isn't just living off the grid; it's living *in* an ever-changing medium that requires constant attention and accommodation. Your perceptions and sensitivity to the ocean and atmosphere will increase dramatically. Like a sommelier and his wine, you will learn to appreciate the subtleties in the physical world around you.

- Sailing a boat on the open ocean demands mastery of many skills. You may not leave with them, but you'll return with them. Your capacity for personal responsibility expands dramatically.

- Traveling slowly (about jogging speed) forces an appreciation for the size and scale of this world not possible by plane or train. Moving at your own pace tests your capacity for creative thought because you invent every experience yourself.

- White sand beaches? You'll find plenty out cruising (in the tropics), and you'll have them all to yourself. You can't get that in Jamaica.

What are Your Life Circumstances?

Every cruiser is *out there* cruising for a different reason, and you don't have to go to psychotherapy, take a personality test, visit a shaman or hypnotherapist, or read self-help books to figure out why you want to go out and bob around on the ocean while everyone else you know continues down the same old path. The _why_ in your life doesn't need to have a complicated answer, just an honest one.

Start by taking a long, hard look at where you are in life, understand what you truly want to get out the cruising experience, and set some specific guidelines for how you imagine accomplishing these nebulous goals in an idealized world. The idea here is to try and reflect on your true motivations and expectations. I'll start.

I should have been more honest with myself

Unfortunately before our first cruise, I never took the time to analyze my true motivations for going and I never gave any thought to what I wanted to get out of cruising. Aside from the financial requirements, I never considered what exactly it would take to make *The Dream* a reality. Only now can I see where this critical self-knowledge would have helped sell my [soon to-be] wife on *The Dream*, and would have made that first cruising experience more successful.

My Dream

When the bug first bit, I was in my late 20's with a successful career as a TV meteorologist in the San Francisco Bay Area. I had some money in the bank, a house, cars, lots of guy toys, and a few close friends that I didn't get to see enough because of my crazy work schedule. Overall, life was pretty good: I could afford what I wanted, people knew me on the street, and I got to spend plenty of quality time with a woman I truly loved.

All I really knew about *my dream* at the time was, "I have been in love with boats and sailing since before I can remember. Cruising a sailboat to distant shores is a natural extension of my love for sailing, travel, and adventure, so I want to do it full-time!" Self-examination never went any further than this.

The truth

The reality that I can see clearly now is much, much different than what I was telling myself at the time: I hated my job; I hated everything about it: getting up at 3 AM, wearing a suit and tie, makeup (yes, really, and plenty of it), and making insincere chit-chat with superficial news anchors while listening to news stories made my stomach turn. Being recognizable as a local celebrity made me self-conscious and uncomfortable when I was out and about.

I had a healthy bank account, but no understanding of my investments or how I was spending my money. I hardly ever saw my friends because of my job. Megan and I spent quality time together, but our working hours prevented less than an hour or so together every day. Too often we complained about the banalities of life. Owning the house, the car, the stuff didn't make me feel free and successful.

Instead, it made me feel trapped and lonely.

The promise

Before that first trip, I saw cruising as an escape, a chance to start over; an opportunity to control my own destiny for a change and be my own boss. The want of travel and adventure were genuine for sure, but the motivations were much deeper than I allowed myself to admit. I wanted to have a closer relationship with Megan. I hoped to develop deep and lasting friendships with like-minded adventurers in distant ports of call. Above all else, I hoped that cruising would change how I experienced life.

In a nutshell, the reality of my life before we went cruising the first time was that I was a lonely, unfulfilled career-aholic who felt trapped by his belongings and life circumstances. I felt as though I wasn't wringing all that I could out of life, and that there just, "has to be more," to all of this. All I really knew for sure was that I wasn't as happy as I thought I should be and sailing away looked like more fun than psychotherapy. Cheaper too.

Now it's your turn

I'm sharing my story here in the hope that you will be honest with yourself about your life circumstances and your motivations for wanting to do something as illogical as setting sail for full-time cruising. If you don't question your motivations at this stage of the game, your wife certainly will when you try to get her to buy into *your dream*. At that point, you need to have some real answers.

Consider some of these questions: Are you happy with your life as it is right now? Is there anything that you are running from? Are you satisfied with your job? Friends? Work/life balance? Do you have societal/community/political reasons for wanting to go? Are there financial reasons for wanting to go cruising?

What Do You Want?

Once you have a good idea for *why* you want to go cruising, let's move on to the question of what you hope to get out of cruising. What are your goals and what are your expectations? What do you want from this experience?

- Adventure?
- Freedom?
- Mastery?
- Solitude?
- Control?
- White sand beaches?
- Romance of the sea?
- Simply indefinable?

Is it something specific like visiting a particular atoll where you're grandfather's plane was shot down in WWII? Do you want to sail around the world just so you can say you did it? Write your answers down.

There are no wrong answers here but these are the <u>right</u> questions. We want your wife to be able to ask the right questions, not answer the wrong questions for herself, which she will do automatically if you aren't open and honest with her.

How Do You Want to Do This?

If you've stewed on the cruising dream for a while, I'm sure you have a rough plan in mind, right? This is the part that keeps you up at night, in a good way. I'm not talking about a specific action plan that will put you on the water at a certain date and time. No, I'm asking if you have a general idea of how you want to go about cruising. Much of this will depend on where you are in life and where you are financially. Is this:

1. Near-term? Perhaps in the next year or two?
2. Long-term? "Some day," as in a few years, or when you retire?

3. A permanent change. "I'm going to change my lifestyle for good and forever."
4. Temporary adventure? "I want to head down to The Islands for the season."

Try to form a clear and specific, but be <u>realistic</u> here as there is no need to idealize. For example, if you are 25 years old with $10,000 in the bank, retiring permanently in a year or two for an open-ended cruise is not realistic. Three months in Mexico? Yes, that could be done easily. Conversely, if you are 85 years old, you can't expect to set off cruising around the world in ten or twenty years. You need to get out soon. (Yes, there are 85-year-olds out sailing around the world, so don't let that stop you.)

Clarify this fantasy as precisely as possible because the more concisely and specifically you define what you want, the easier it will be for your wife to understand. The better she understands, the less her objections will be based on confusion. So let's try to be specific; what follows are some *typical* cruising fantasies...I mean plans:

1. **Local sailing**. You are not interested in voyaging at all right now, but would like to get involved in local sailing and take the occasional charter. Beyond that, you are open to seeing where life takes you. You might be interested in cruising full time later on, but there is no need to decide now. You would be happy to own your own boat and enjoy sailing with your wife.

2. **Part-time or a sabbatical.** You like the idea of a part-time cruising lifestyle filled with, "mini-retirements," or sabbaticals of two to three months. You enjoy life ashore. You have stable finances and can afford to take longer stretches for yourself. Your job or career allows you to come and go or work remotely. You want to get out and cruise, but aren't ready to ditch your life on land.

3. **Full-time but temporary cruising lifestyle.** You like the idea of a one to five-year plan to cruise the Pacific, the Caribbean, the Med, or around the world. You won't hang on to your job, and maybe not even your career, but you are fine with that. It's time to re-boot anyway. You could keep the house, cars, and stuff if it makes sense financially, but cutting those nets away is pretty attractive too. You're ready to drop everything, but know you will be back one day.

4. **Full retirement.** "I'm done." This is the open-ended, full-time cruise in which you may or may not ever come back. No need to hang onto the house and junk because if you do swallow the anchor in a few years, you aren't moving back to Toledo. Financially, there is no need to worry about the future; the bills are paid until the day you die. You're never coming back.

Focus on the ideal plan based on where you are in your life today, because "someday" never really comes. As you'll see below, ambiguity and unrealistic expectations will limit your wife's involvement and keep you at the dock.

Case Studies

Let me tell you about a few of the future cruisers / dreamers I've met along the way that you might be able to relate to. The names and some other key facts have been changed of course to protect anonymity, but I can assure you that these people are 100% real. They are included here because they convinced me that they were not just committed to the cruising dream, but that they were actively taking steps to make it a reality.

Barry

Barry is about 50 years old and owns an old wooden 65 footer at the end of the dock. With the long bowsprit, the boat is closer to 80 feet. It's a classic; very high style with a complicated looking gaff-ketch rig. He's owned this, "work in progress," for 15 years and he's down on the boat at least three weekday afternoons/evenings and both Saturday and Sunday. He's usually working on a complicated woodworking project and has a full compliment of tools on the boat, in his car, and at home. He is a craftsman and his work is flawless.

Barry has talked about his wife on many occasions, but neither Megan nor I have ever seen her. In the year that we lived on our boat down by Barry's, his was only out sailing once. He talked about the trip for weeks.

In general, Barry is a friendly guy. He enjoys talking boats, equipment, and gear with any passer-by. He's shared his plan with Megan and I and it goes something like this: he has another ten years of working for the City of Oakland ahead of him, which will give him just enough time to finish his long list of projects on the boat. "She'll be ready by then!" He is an avid reader and quotes Steinbeck about the Sea of Cortez, which he plans on visiting before taking the boat to the South Pacific. When does he plan on coming back? "Never."

Will his wife Mary come along for the trip? Well she, "doesn't like the boat," which she calls Barry's, "mistress." Does he want her to come along on the cruise? "It's up to her."

Marty

Marty is a 30-something software sales engineer. He has a J-24 that he bought with the intention of doing some beer-can races with the guys out in front of the Berkeley Pier. He loves sailing the boat, but racing turned out to be too much trouble: tuning the boat to be competitive was expensive, getting and keeping crew was a hassle, and taking time off work to get down to prep the boat for races took time away from his wife who he loves very much.

We've seen his wife Sarah down on the dock often drinking a beer and hanging out, but according to Marty, she has no interest in sailing. It was, "too wet and uncomfortable that one time we went out." He doesn't want to push her into it.

Marty wants to move up to a bigger J-boat (another racer) in the next couple of years. Further down the road when he has his finances together, he'd like to get *out there* and cruise, "maybe on a 45-footer." He says, "those Swans sure are beautiful, and fast too!"

Would he sail more often if his wife wanted to come along? "I'd be out here every weekend, probably more," he says.

Jim and Emily

Jim and Emily are in their late 40s and are, "getting ready," to make the big jump to full-time liveaboard status. They bought their Hunter 45 two boat shows ago, and have loaded her up with the latest and greatest gear. They have everything from washer and dryer to a closed circuit camera system for security. They keep the boat spotless.

Jim comes down to the marina once a week by himself and usually has a cart full of bags from West Marine. He and his wife spend most weekends on the boat, frequently with friends. They take the boat out occasionally (once a month or so), but dockside entertainment is their favorite pastime.

Jim and Emily are outgoing people who seem happy, laughing and joking with each other constantly. Unfortunately, the mood changes drastically when they are coming and going from their slip. We can hear Jim yelling and screaming [often contradictory] orders from more than 100 yards away. Emily retorts with her own directions for his work at the helm. More than a couple of times we heard (and felt) the crunch of the dock against their shiny new hull. Usually, after they got the engine shut down, we'd witness a lot of silent, purposeful hull cleaning and stainless polishing.

I didn't ever get their complete story, but apparently they are either independently wealthy or are entrepreneurs of some sort. For whatever reason, we think that they're financially able to head off for a cruise any time they wanted to. They never do, in fact they never even move aboard their boat full time in the year that we live in that marina. "Maybe next month."

Ely (and Lisa)

Ely is almost 40, and he's never owned a boat. I took him out on my Merit 25 day sailor/racer a couple of times, and he's obviously smitten by sailing and the idea of cruising. He's got some money and works in a profession that would allow him employment whenever and wherever he wanted it (he's a senior software engineer). Unfortunately, his fiancé Lisa won't hear anything about buying a boat, even to sail on the bay.

When we bought our Peterson 46, *Low Pressure* and told Ely that we planned to head out for a five-year cruise, he said something like, "I would die to do something like that, but I can't even get my wife to go camping."

Are you one of these guys?

You probably know a Barry or a Marty or Jim or Ely. You might even be one of them yourself. Maybe you can relate to some part of their stories or a combination of two. I've personally met dozens of dreamers like these guys. They are putting one step in front of the other, trying to set their plans for a life of freedom and adventure into action, but *The Dream* is going nowhere:

- Barry can't go because his boat is too big to run by himself and his wife isn't interested in doing boat work.

- Marty can't go because his wife doesn't enjoy sailing.

- Jim and Emily can't go because sailing makes them hate each other.
- Ely can't go (can't even buy a boat) because he waits for his wife's approval to take any step forward.

The sad truth is that I met all of these people before our first cruise eight years ago, and I checked in with them recently. Not one of them is any closer to going cruising. Even poor Ely is no closer to owning his own bay-sailor. Yes, Lisa is now his wife.

What's Standing in Your Way?

Reading those brief descriptions above, you might be thinking: "it's her fault; our wives keep us men from doing what we want...they are the ones that hold us back...if it weren't for my wife, I'd just buy that boat and sail away." These are convenient excuses and flawed thinking that keep us from facing our own fears.

The truth is that Barry could buy a smaller boat that didn't require 25 years of preparation; a boat that didn't alienate his wife. Marty could buy a boat that allowed an acceptably level of safety and comfort for his wife. Jim and Emily could learn to work together to run the boat without so much stress. Even poor Ely could move forward without his wife's direct approval. Better yet, any of these gentlemen could employ the tactics in this book to get their wives on board before they ever bought a boat.

Excuses

Before we spend a lot of time and effort getting your wife on board, let's make sure you don't have any personal issues standing in the way of *your dream*. If you have the cruising bug, I mean really have a yearning to put to sea and test yourself with extended voyages to distant landfalls, why aren't you off doing it or making plans to do it right now?

When we told our "someday" cruising friends that we had set a date to cut the dock lines and go, inevitably (and without prompting) they'd give reasons why they weren't going too. Here are the most common reasons men give for not going now:

1. "I/we don't have enough money."
2. "I/we don't have enough experience."
3. "My wife isn't into it."

The first two reasons are lame excuses as I'll talk about below. The last reason is absolutely legitimate, but really only points to the real reason you don't go. We'll spend the rest of this book solving this problem.

Money

Finances are a poor excuse for not going. The reality is that almost anyone [in a developed country] can set off cruising virtually anytime they want. Seriously. If you could drum up even $15k (sell your car and get a part-time bartending job for six months), you could sail from any east-coast port and spend most of a season in the Caribbean without touching the credit cards. Granted the boat would be simple and small, and the food and drink would be staples, but it could be done. The same thing goes for any west-coast sailor heading for Mexico, and in fact it could be done for $10k or even slightly less.

I know what you're thinking: these numbers look ridiculously low; unbelievably low in fact. Yet there are plenty of safe little sailboats sitting in your local marina that could be purchased for just a few thousand. Hit a Costco for a stock of rice and beans, and outfit your ride with some basic safety and navigation equipment. Starting with nothing, you could go in just a few months, no problem.

Buy the same simple little boat and add $10k to your cruising budget and you are living in the lap of luxury for a season down-island, likely the most memorable season you'll spend in your entire life. No, money is not what holds people back.

Experience

There is a misconception among "someday" cruisers that there is a certain level of aptitude or ability or experience or whatever you want to call it that must be attained before you head off cruising. While you certainly need to know how to handle the conditions expected on the voyage and should have some idea how to repair or jury-rig things that commonly break, the truth is that you will <u>never</u> know everything there is to know about voyaging. The ocean (as well as your boat) will continue to teach you lessons in your tenth or twentieth year.

The only fundamental requirement is that you have a level of competence and experience that allows you to overcome your <u>fears</u>. The rest of it will take care of itself along the way. You will deal with things as they happen, and you will learn as you go.

The real reason most don't go now

Though few will admit to even their closest friends, <u>fear</u> is the real reason most would-be cruisers don't go now. That fear can manifest in a myriad of ways: insecurity over loosing your social standing in your community, fear of losing your career, fear of not having money for the "future," etc. Fear can also express itself as anxiety over being alone, fear of the ocean, or fear of death itself. These are all really one fear: <u>fear of the unknown. It's intolerance for ambiguity that keeps most in port.</u>

Many men unconsciously transfer their own fear or intolerance for ambiguity onto their wives.

In this final part of a chapter on self-examination, it's critical that you take a long hard look at whether your wife is really what stands between you and your dream. It's entirely possible that your own fears are what keep your boat in its slip and put your cruising dream in the realm of, "some day."

Your Wife is the Key

Instead of seeing your wife or *her* fears as an impediment to achieving *your dream*, it's time to look at her as the number one most important asset you have right now that can make this whole silly thing possible. She is everything you need to make this happen.

Not only is she a potentially valuable crewmember, helping with the day-to-day and hour-to-hour operation of the boat, but more importantly you and your wife together have a much better chance of conquering those paralyzing fears that keep most dreamers in port.

Your wife is an infinite source of power, strength and reinforcing determination. She has the power to inspire you; the ability to prop you up when you need it. She'll cut the loneliness from a dark night. She'll help you focus your efforts toward the goal. She'll quiet your questioning mind. Your wife is the key to turning your dream into a reality. Just as in life ashore, the two of you together are stronger and more capable than as individuals apart.

But first we have to get her on board.

3.
About Your Wife

In the last chapter we got to know you a little better; we have essential information about you: what your motivations are, what you want to get from the cruising experience, and what your ideal cruising plan looks like. Keep that information in mind. In this chapter, we are going to consider the other 50% of this cruising partnership; your wife. We'll clarify:

- ✓ What you want and expect from her.
- ✓ Her talents and how they fit into *The Dream*.
- ✓ What motivates her.
- ✓ Her tolerance for risk and ambiguity.

Bookstore shelves are filled with countless titles written on the differences between men and women. Recreating and rehashing *Vogue Magazine* articles about what makes her tick or how to have a more fulfilling relationship are not the goals here.   Instead in this chapter I'll help you assess your potential partner in light of the differences between men and women as they pertain to the requirements of a seagoing life.

Ignorance is no excuse

When I first became infected with *the cruising dream*, I was 28 years old. I didn't know what I didn't know, and that applied to my wife as much as it did to myself. You might be quick to blame my ignorance on being young and dumb, but having now met many, many captains of all ages whose wives are or were standing in the way of *The Dream*, I can tell you that age has nothing to do with it.

The primary reason that so few of us are able to get her on board is that we don't take the time to understand her motivations, fears, capabilities and tolerance for risk and ambiguity. We need to answer these questions: What are we going to ask from her? What do we have to work with? Where is she in her life emotionally? We need to do some recon.

What Do You Want from Her?

Please, please, please know what you are asking from your wife before you start talking about an endless vacation or buying a boat; you need to be as clear and specific as possible about your vision for her in *The Dream*. If you aren't clear about your expectations, her reaction will be based automatically on an imagined worst-case scenario, which in her mind could be an endless, non-stop voyage on a tiny, dirty old boat, never to return.

So let's get specific. Her role in each of the following scenarios completely re-defines how you'll approach her, what she may object to, and why she'll commit. You want:

1. Support at home while you go off sailing and cruising by yourself (I sure hope this isn't your plan).

2. Companionship for recreational sailing in your local area.

3. Part-time cruising companion. She joins you for specific legs of the trip.

4. She joins the boat as full-time live aboard crew for a defined period.

5. She joins the boat for an indefinite period on an open-ended retirement cruise.

The last thing you want is to give your wife too many options. If you ask your hesitant wife to <u>choose</u> among these scenarios, you'll likely end up with unmentioned option 6, which is "none of the above." Trustworthy captains inspire support by stating clear objectives, and this my friend is the first and best opportunity to start practicing.

What will she do?

Successful cruising couples find a way to work in partnership to run the boat. As we'll talk about in Chapter 8, those that get *out there* and stay *out there* settle into separate and defined roles; yet they work cooperatively. Where does your wife fit into the operational aspects of cruising as you see it now? What level of participation are you expecting (imagining) from her when she's on board? Today, do you see her as a/an:

1. Equal partner? She will do everything that you do on board, including maintenance, navigation, pilotage, routing, weather forecasting, etc. She is as capable a skipper as you are.

2. Competent crew? She knows how to do most tasks and works the boat independently from you while she's on watch. You continue to assume a leadership role while she follows your direction.

3. Incompetent crew? She takes all direction from you in every operation. She will stand watch by herself but you'll be called on watch if sails need trimming or the

course altered. You handle all maintenance issues yourself.

4. Passenger? She will cook and clean and probably help with the cosmetic upkeep of the boat, but you plan on handling every other aspect of running the boat. She may not even stand watch by herself.

Are your expectations realistic?

Many men mistakenly assume that if she cooks the food and stands a short watch or two, he'll be able to handle absolutely everything else on the boat. This is a common and largely unrealistic plan that leads to a lot of shortened itineraries and abandoned boats, and it's not because he can't handle the boat on his own.

Regardless of what she might say, your wife needs and wants to do more than just cook, clean, and read in her bunk. Does that sound fun anyway? Not for most women. "Allowing" her to sit there passively while you do all the work may be appreciated initially, but she will get bored, and as we'll talk about later, boredom kills The Dream faster than anything else.

She must remain stimulated to stay interested, and that means she has to participate. The good news is that sailing, by its nature is very "hands on" and your wife will have endless opportunities to develop new skills to actively participate in running the boat.

It's equally unrealistic to expect your wife to be an equally contributing partner right away. Even if she were interested and motivated to take on all the same responsibilities that you have, it will take time and patience to learn. To set your expectations correctly, you need to think carefully about your wife in ways that you may not have had to before.

What Do We Have to Work with Here?

Aside from the obvious, like boating experience or how comfortable she is on the water, we need to know a few things about your wife, and this falls into roughly two categories: technical aptitude and ability as well as emotional capacity and flexibility. While emotional capacity and flexibility are much more important to *the cruising dream* than skill or aptitude, it turns out that the latter feeds into the former; the more she is able to actively participate in running the boat, the greater her emotional capacity and flexibility will be when things aren't going well. In other words, the more she knows, the less she will fear.

Character traits

Here are a few other things to consider: is she a curious person? Does she have the desire to learn new things? Is she strong willed? Is she physically fit? Is she strong? Is she patient, or does she become frustrated easily? Where does she channel her creativity?

Existing talents and skills

When I first started hinting to Megan that I had *The Dream*, she didn't have any experience on sailboats at all. None. She didn't express any fear of the water per-se, but she was afraid of the ocean (storms and worst-case scenarios). She didn't play any sports, but had enjoyed competitive tennis and soccer when she was younger. She was physically fit, but not strong.

Megan had no sailing skills, but she did have some technical skills that were invaluable once we did get going with *The Dream*, and her abilities complemented areas where I was deficient. She was:

1. Very organized and clean.
2. An amateur seamstress, sewing from patterns and from scratch.
3. Good with administrative tasks.

These particular skills are very useful on a cruising boat. Staying organized on a boat is a monumental task that requires structure, constant adjustment, and an eye for detail. I call Megan the, "Google of Boat Stuff," because she could find just about anything on the boat at any time when I asked, "do you know where that _____ is?"

Cleanliness is imperative when you live in such a small space; unnecessary clutter and dirt takes a toll on the crew's morale. On the few occasions where I did live on the boat alone for a few days, it only took an hour or two to become a disaster zone, and usually cleaned only an hour or two before her return. Megan's eye for rooting out dirt was amazing, adding immeasurably to the livability of the space.

Megan's talents with a sewing machine saved us thousands of dollars. She completely re-upholstered the boat inside and out. She repaired sails, replaced luff-tape on two jibs, and even made a full-boat cover (*Low Pressure* was just over 50 ft.) that weighed more than she did. She made custom bags, cockpit shades, deck shades, lee cloths, and dozens of other custom doo-dads that added immeasurably to the comfort and safety of the boat.

There are a surprising number of administrative tasks when you are running a small boat, and Megan kept the paperwork in order. From watching our finances, corresponding with home, keeping track of other cruisers and social obligations (and there will be plenty) check in and check out procedures in foreign ports, parts lists, repair lists, and provisioning lists; Megan's abilities to manage these duties kept our administrative ship afloat on both cruises.

Teaching and learning

There are going to be a lot of lessons to learn. This can either be a lot of fun and part of the joy of voyaging, or it can be painful at every turn. How good a student is your wife? Did she do well in school? Was she studious or did she mostly wing it? Was she a bookworm, or did she need hands-on instruction?

If she is/was an interested and curious student, she'll have an easier time getting over the primary hurdle that most women face in setting off on an adventure like this: fear. As we'll talk about throughout the book, but especially in Chapter 8, knowledge conquers fear. The more adept she is at learning, the faster her anxieties will fade.

Strength and fitness

If there's one aspect of your wife that will have the greatest impact on her day-to-day *enjoyment* of the cruising experience, it is her physical fitness and strength. You may not realize just how much bending, lifting, hauling, etc, are involved in the everyday voyaging life. In fact, this is not an activity to undertake if you are not in shape.

You certainly don't have to be an athlete, but you do have to have the strength to carry 50 lb. jerry jugs, lift bulk food out of the dingy, and be able to grind the mainsail up or bring in a big jib sheet. If your wife (or you) is grossly overweight or not physically fit for whatever reason, cruising is going to be a lot less enjoyable, probably painful, certainly more dangerous, and will add an unnecessary element of risk.

When one of you has a debilitating physical illness or injury, not only do all of the operational duties fall on the other person, but care for the sick crew will take time and energy as well. It's important that both of you be in good condition before setting of on your journey.

During our first cruise, I was the fitness liability, not my wife. I was in good condition overall, but had a nagging back problem for a few years. What during our life ashore was temporary soreness and mild discomfort quickly became completely debilitating and ultimately incapacitating aboard our boat.

Over a few months of full-time cruising, soreness progressed to muscle spasms and sciatica. Finally in San Carlos, Mexico, a disk in my lower back ruptured. I was in agonizing pain and completely immobilized for about a week.

In that time, Megan managed to strip the entire boat of canvas and do about 99% of the work needed to put the boat on the hard for the five months of hurricane season. She did it, but she was not happy.

Creativity

Is she creative? We've spoken a little bit about sailing and cruising as your art; the way you express yourself and create something of value. Let's apply the same line of thought to your wife. What is her art? How does she express herself creatively? Does she scrapbook? Build decks? Dance? Yoga? Garden? What are her creative outlets?

If cruising offers one thing above all else, it is time; time to slow down and do whatever you want to do. If your wife enjoys writing, photography, or some other creative, time consuming activity, cruising is an awesome opportunity to squeeze those creative juices. If she doesn't have any hobbies or other creative outlets, this can become a liability as boredom sets in after your twentieth white sand beach destination.

Cruising often requires creative solutions to unexpected problems. Creative people have a definite advantage when it comes to dealing with unforeseen circumstances. If your wife is creative, she'll have a much easier time rolling with the inevitable punches, contributing important insights, and participating in running the boat to determining where, how, and when things will happen.

Attitude

A "live and learn," attitude is critical to a successful cruise. Does your wife make lemonade out of lemons? Is she a glass half full, or glass half empty sort of person? Is she basically hopeful and optimistic or pessimistic and cynical? Her inclination (like yours) towards positivity is a fundamental pillar to the success of this endeavor.

Her age may have a significant bearing on whether your wife is optimistic in general. In a study of 9,800 people over the age of 50 conducted by Dr. Elizabeth Breeze at the University College of London, women become more optimistic and enjoy life more as they age. It appears that maturity is important in keeping a smile on her face when the weather turns sour or equipment breaks.

The good news is that a positive outlook on life can be cultivated. Having gratitude for what you have right now is the best way to improve your attitude. Cruising will change some of the factors that influence attitude: "keeping up with the Jones's is meaningless while out cruising. Not only will almost all comparison with friends, neighbors, family, and coworkers disappear completely, but in many third-world countries, you will see just how fortunate you are to have what you have.

Aesthetics

Women place a much higher emphasis and importance on physical attractiveness than men do. I know what you're saying to yourself: we are the shallow pigs who care most about looks while women care most about personality. While that is true when it comes to physical attraction and finding a mate, in every other situation, women are more concerned with the aesthetics of things while men are much more interested in functionality.

Your wife is going to be much more critical of the way the

boat looks than you are. For you, the beauty of a boat is not just in the lines, the color scheme, or how crisp and new the sails look. For you the beauty of the boat lies in its functionality, the engineering, and the quality of the materials used. Your wife is much more interested in the cushions matching the throw pillows. Where you can talk for days about the charging system, the radar arch, and the watermaker's capability, she is much more interested in whether the brightwork looks good or if the stainless is stain-less.

Her aesthetic sense applies to herself as well; she is more concerned with her physical appearance than you are. She probably doesn't equate sailing with a "good hair day," so it may be difficult for your wife to imagine that she'll be able to keep up her physical appearance while out cruising. She sees the boat as a place to, "rough it." Her tolerance for this will change over time, but it will be helpful for you to understand that her need to look and feel beautiful is primal.

You need to stay attractive too. Studies have shown that she is as much afraid that your looks will decline with age as she is that your bank account will suffer. On racing boats, grown men go without a shower for a week without a complaint. She is not going to tolerate this. Research has shown that your wife is more sensitive to bad smells than you are. (This might explain why men think farts are funnier than women.)

How well does she sleep?

She is more sensitive to sounds than you are. Some research has shown that you are more sensitive to low-frequency sound, but across every other audible wavelength, she is more sensitive.

This may explain why women sometimes have difficulty getting good rest aboard a boat. Boats make noise: wind in the rigging, waves lapping at the hull, creaky bulkheads, slatting sails, the anchor snubber, etc. Additionally, cruising is living on and <u>in</u> the ocean, and the ocean is a noisy place. You will hear all sorts of sound from shrimp, clams, fish, dolphins, whales, etc., transmitted through the hull and into the living space. It is good to consider ahead of time what her threshold is for resting in a less than silent environment.

Emotional Recon

I'm sure it's no surprise to hear that your wife is much more in touch with her emotions than you are, but as it applies to *The Dream* of cruising, many men make the mistake of oversimplifying her emotional needs and not understanding what I'll call her *emotional flexibility*. We need to understand where your wife falls on the emotional spectrum, how this compares to your emotional spectrum, and how flexible she is from her baseline state in specific key areas.

Things and goals

You value objects, things, attaining goals, successes, and accomplishment. Those things are important to her as well, but what she *values* above those things are: love, communication, and relationships. The differences between your core values and hers is easily ignored or adapted to in your life ashore, but when it comes to *The Dream*, these differences are like night and day.

Independence

Everyone is an individual, but in general men want status and independence while women want intimacy and connection most. Where does your wife fall on this spectrum? How independent is she? Does she have to run every decision by a committee of her peers or does she arrive at her own decisions by herself? Is your mother-in-law on the phone to help make sure the recipe is followed correctly or does your wife take the initiative with a dash of this and a sprinkle of that? Is your wife a leader of her tribe or a follower?

Self-sufficiency is a very macho concept, and *The Dream* is probably the ultimate expression of independence: this is an activity where you are responsible for absolutely every aspect of the venture. Your wife on the other hand may not place as much value in being alone, independent, and self-sufficient. She may be much more attracted to the communal aspects of cruising.

The great thing about cruising is that it delivers on both fronts. The reality is that there are very few cruisers who are *out there* alone, seeking solitude at every turn. Between our two cruises, we met only one couple that shunned the herd mentality completely and set off on their own path at every opportunity. They were not particularly sociable with other cruisers, preferring to make connections with the locals that they met along the way. For the vast majority of cruisers out there *doing it*, the cruising community is one of strong, lasting bonds.

Motivation

What motivates your wife? It's likely very different from what motivates you. You are motivated by the problem that needs solving. You see a need and you are drawn to filling it. You are even more motivated when you feel that you yourself are needed, necessary, and an integral part of the solution. Is there a problem that needs fixing? Bilge alarm going off? You're on it. The main halyard banging on the mast at 3am? You spring out of your berth in your underwear. After you are done fixing the transmission or bending on a sail, you need to receive appreciation, admiration, and approval for a job well done.

In contrast, she is motivated when she feels special, cherished, and, "loved." Is there a problem that needs fixing? Don't just give her the solution and don't simply tell her what to do. She wants to be heard, understood, and encouraged *before* the task is undertaken. When she is done, she wants respect and validation if it went well and understanding and reassurance if it hasn't gone well. We'll talk a lot more about motivation in Chapters 5 and 8.

Big-picture thinking

Is your wife super focused, or is she a big-picture thinker? Men typically have laser focus. When we decide on a target, goal, program or plan, we put the blinders on and set out to accomplish it. We don't need to ask everyone in our circle for advice and we hate asking for directions.

She doesn't have the same blinders and laser focus that you do; instead of a laser pointer, she has a flood lamp. She is holistic and integrative in her approach. She is a planner, tending to focus more on long-term goals. When you bring up the idea of the five-year cruise, she is already thinking about where you two will live afterward.

Your wife is very good at integrating vastly disparate pieces of the puzzle together in her mind. This talent for big-picture thinking can yield valuable insights, but she may also have a tendency to jump to conclusions. This fact alone is what makes it so difficult for men to convince their wives to go cruising: with an ambiguous plan in hand, they face a litany of pre-conceived ideas at every turn. We'll develop specific strategies to work around this in the next chapter.

Fear and insecurity

I've saved the best and most important for last: we need to know how tolerant your wife is of risk and ambiguity. What do I mean by this? I mean _how does she react in the face of an uncertain future?_

News flash: sailing and cruising involve unavoidable risk to safety and welfare, to finances and career, etc. The risks are small and in this author's opinion well worth the reward, however it is **risk and ambiguity** that forms the basis for most wives' objections to *The Cruising Dream*. Her tolerance for risk is much different than yours.

Risk

Women are somewhat more risk-averse than men. In a 1989 *Survey of Consumer Finances* sponsored by the Federal Reserve System, each of the 3,143 respondents was asked the following question: "Which of these statements comes closest to the amount of financial risk that you (and your husband/wife) are willing to take when you save or make investments?"

1. Will take *substantial* financial risk expecting to earn *substantial* returns,
2. Will take *above average* financial risks expecting to earn *above average* returns,
3. Will take *average* financial risks expecting to earn *average* returns, or
4. *Not* willing to take any financial risks.

Roughly 60% of the female respondents said they were not willing to accept <u>any</u> risk, while only 40% of the men said they were unwilling to take <u>any</u> risks. What this tells us is that she is *somewhat* more risk-averse than you are, but overall there isn't a tremendous difference.

Ambiguity

What is more important, surprising, and useful to getting your wife on board is that while women are *somewhat* more risk-averse than men, study after study has determined that women are much, much more *ambiguity*-averse than men. What does that mean? <u>Women need to have a plan</u>.

While you or I are much more comfortable with the idea of casting our lines off for whatever adventure on the high seas may come our way, our wives want to know when, where, how long, and at what cost. Women are much more uncomfortable with an uncertain or ambiguous future than men. So it isn't so much the risk she may object to, it's not knowing the outcome. There is a big difference between risk and ambiguity.

Other research has shown that a woman's tolerance for *ambiguity* (unknown or unknowable future) goes up with increasing *competence*. This means that the more she knows about something, the more she is willing to tolerate an unknown or unknowable outcome. This will be a key part of our strategy in getting her onboard; the more she knows about cruising and sailing, the greater the chance she'll tolerate the risks and ambiguities involved.

One final study I'll share by Riley and Chow (1992) found risk aversion to decline with wealth, education, and age, until age 65, at which time risk aversion increases. All women are different, but at the end of the day, you are going to have the easiest time convincing your wife to go cruising if she is middle aged, educated, and wealthy.

Conclusion

Every woman is unique, but if you hope to have any chance of *getting her on board*, your wife needs to hear that you have a specific plan. That plan in turn depends on where you see her fitting into *your dream*. By understanding what is required of her as a member of the team and where her strengths, abilities, talents, fears, and motivations lie, you can better lead her into an unknown and unknowable future.

4.

The Approach

We need to grease this one on fellas...there's a lot riding on the landing.

In general, people tend to fall into categories: there are leaders and followers, dreamers and realists, saints and sinners, optimists and cynics, etc. Most relevant to this book are drivers and passengers. I'm a driver: I like to steer the car, take the helm of a boat, and handle the yoke of an aircraft. I am going to assume that you are a driver too, so I think you'll appreciate the following analogy. In aviation we talk about the *phases* of flight:

1. taxi,
2. take-off run,
3. take-off,
4. climb,
5. cruise,
6. descent,
7. approach,
8. landing,
9. roll-out,

Of those phases of flight, two are far more dangerous than the others, and are referred to as "critical" phases: take-off and landing. This is when the aircraft is most vulnerable, the margin of error is smallest and where most accidents occur; the aircraft is moving relatively slowly (the wings are least efficient) and is closest to the ground. Not many things have to go wrong in a *critical* phase of flight for a catastrophic result.

To minimize the dangers and prepare for any malfunctions or unforeseen circumstances during these *critical* phases of flight, the pilot checks and double-checks systems, procedures, and parameters during the operations <u>preceding</u> the critical phases of flight: the take-off run and the approach. If anything looks out of the ordinary: acceleration not right, surface winds unstable, engines not performing to spec, etc. while the plane rolls down the runway gaining speed, we make the decision to abort the take-off.

Alternatively, if things don't look quite right as we make our approach to the airport: not aligned with the runway, above or below the glide path, or going too fast or too slow, the pilot will abort the landing, and make a "missed approach." By taking decisive action *before* we are in a critical situation, we avert an accident and live to try again.

The same principles apply to getting your wife on board. Pitching your wife (next chapter) on the cruising dream is very much a critical phase of flight. To assure success, we are going to put extra effort and emphasis on perfecting the approach.

Why Many Crash and Burn

Most men don't fully appreciate how foreign a concept this *cruising dream* is for their wives. While your wife may agree that the idea of cruising sounds fun or interesting, she may not actually believe you would ever go through with it – it's just so, "far out." For these wives, cruising is an abstraction or conceptualization at the very most. When their husbands take the next step and propose that they actually go ahead and move forward (buy a boat, move aboard, cut the dock lines, or whatever the next step might be), she is suddenly confronted with a reality that she had to that point denied might actually manifest.

If he doesn't notice or realize that the approach has gone awry and continues with the landing by buy buying a boat or deciding to move aboard, she may never get on board with *The Dream* itself. Going back for another try becomes difficult or impossible.

Skip the tricks

When and if she resists this next step, he may resort to learned manipulative behaviors that might be affective for getting what he wants in day-to-day life ashore, but absolutely disastrous for *the cruising dream.* A female sailing instructor I interviewed for this book related some of the following quotes she's heard from women (from their husbands' mouths) in her sailing programs.

- "I've worked my whole life to build a home for you, now you owe me this."
- "I'm buying a boat and going cruising. You're welcome to come along if you'd like."
- "You can stay here alone, but you better get a job."
- "I'm going with or without you."

Manipulation through guilt or bullying isn't just unethical; it's ineffective when it comes to something like cruising because the venture is more or less under continual reevaluation. If you are able to get her *out there* without getting her on board with *The Dream*, it won't be for very long.

You can't convince her forever

Let's also get rid of all notions of, "convincing," your wife to go cruising. You may be able to convince her to buy a boat, or convince her to go down the coast with you, or convince her of some other tangible sailing goal. Getting her to take the "next step" may just work, but if you go down this path, you will be in the convincing business throughout the entire endeavor. Continually overcoming her resistance is going to get tiresome and tedious. You'll develop resentments that eat away at *The Dream* from the inside.

She's a tough customer

It's not surprising that men so often resort to guilt or bullying or convincing their wives to go cruising. "Selling," *The Dream* to your wife is a daunting task. She can be a tough sell on anything; but when it comes to giving up her life to follow you onto a little boat, she is about the toughest kind of customer:

1. She is not in the market for what you're selling,
2. She doesn't know why she would ever need what you are selling, and
3. She probably doesn't even understand *what* you are selling or even *why* you are selling it.

Because we know intuitively that it's a tough sell, and because we men can be very narrow-minded (focused) and impatient (motivated) two common tactics emerge:

A. Wear her down through the repeat soft-sell, "honey it will be so great, please can we buy a boat and go cruising?" or

B. The hard-sell, "honey, I'm buying a boat and going cruising, whether you like it or not! I want you to come, but I'll go alone."

Sometimes these tactics work and sometimes they don't but either way, she won't be on board with *The Dream* itself. If a boat is purchased without her full buy-in, she will always see it through disapproving eyes, and selling her on it will be that much harder down the road when each subsequent step becomes another opportunity for her objections and the cycle of convincing and manipulation.

Two Approaches in Practice

I've gotten my wife Megan on board twice now. The first time, I approached with tactic A (from above). For a solid 18 months, I hinted, hassled, whined, bribed, guilted, and tried every which way to convince her how great cruising would be. I told her how the experience would be so liberating, life changing, etc., etc. I came up with itineraries and plans, showed her pretty pictures in magazines, books, and videos. I worked on her at every opportunity, but she wouldn't budge.

Frustrated, I resorted to tactic B and gave her an ultimatum: "Ok then, I'm going to go with or without you," I said, holding back a tear. This was my last volley; my last bullet in the chamber. She didn't answer right away, but in a day or so said, "alright, let's do it."

Yeah! I won! MY DREAM COMES TRUE! HURRAY!

Great news, right? Not so. The underlying premise that she had "caved in" haunted me for the rest of the trip. Because she had never bought into *The Dream* and made it her own, every challenge was an opportunity to reevaluate *my* ̂ decision and voice her disapproval without ever taking responsibility for her part in the decision to go. Because she had never bought in, she was a passenger, not an owner. I was on my own, and was always reminded of the fact at the worst times.

In my second approach to cruising four years later, I changed my entire strategy. Before I ever mentioned a boat or another cruise to Megan, I:

1. Spent as much time as I could with her.
2. Created as many pleasurable situations and interactions as possible, mostly doing what *she* likes to do.

3. Focused on our commonalities instead of our differences: our passions for entrepreneurship and health.
4. Got her involved in my life and had her help me change my diet and exercise routine. Both of us did more physical activities (hiking, etc.) together.
5. Made sure we were getting along beautifully in our relationship.

In the months prior to approaching her again, I changed my own behavior and my interactions in the relationship: when things went wrong in our daily life (noisy construction next door, dishonest business partner), I stayed positive and smiled at my own mistakes with humility. I showed her leadership in adopting new habits and lifestyle elements concurrent with the values that cruising teaches. Still I never talked about boats or cruising.

When the time did come I pitched the cruising subject with confidence and only when the circumstances were absolutely perfect and we were both in the right mental state. Not only did she say yes, she bought into *The Dream* in a way that was missing on the first trip. The results are the inspiration for this book. I want the same thing for you.

The Right Approach

No matter what your dream holds: a short cruise on a small boat, a long cruise on a big boat, or something in between, you've got to have the right approach to get her on board with your dream. If you understand nothing else in this book, I need you to learn and memorize these principles before you begin the approach:

1. Be likeable
2. Confidence is key
3. Always in neutral territory
4. Find emotional stability

If you can set up your approach perfectly, you are two-thirds of the way to a safe and comfortable landing. If not, be ready to give the engines full power and go around for another try when conditions are more favorable. You'll have endless opportunities to try again, but crashing once can ruin future opportunities.

Be Likeable

If you are in a normal, healthy relationship, you probably don't (at least I hope you don't) think of your wife as a sales prospect, but when it comes to selling her on *The Dream* however, you're going to have to change the way you see her, at least for a little while.

Any sales trainer will tell you that when you are trying to sell something, you must develop rapport with your customer; your prospect must like you. In a loving relationship, it is understood and assumed that you *like* each other. However if you are past the honeymoon period (which by the way would be an excellent time to bring up *The Dream*) of about six to nine months of living together, marriage, or full commitment, the amount that you *like* each other varies from time to time. There is nothing inherently wrong with this-it is perfectly normal.

There are natural rhythmic cycles of likeability in any relationship varying from a baseline level, but make no mistake; your likeability is absolutely controllable. These are the tactics we'll use to increase your likeability and thus your influence in your marriage:

1. Use pleasurable association
2. Be there and be present
3. Find common ground
4. Use reciprocal affection
5. Make her feel good
6. Get her to do something for you
7. Smile at your own mistakes
8. Stay positive

"Welcome home honey, I had such a great day; how was yours?" "Can I take your coat?" "Dinner is waiting for you on the table and I'm just drawing you a warm bath..." Don't worry, we aren't going to resort to pandering. The following psychological techniques work primarily on her subconscious. She'll only notice how much closer and attracted she is to you and what you might have to say.

Pleasurable association

When we are in a pleasurable circumstance with someone else, we will associate those feelings with that person. This is one reason why we take our wives to a nice restaurant on the first date. By showing her a good time, she associates pleasurable activities (positive feelings) with us. If you've been in this committed relationship for some time, you'll benefit from taking the initiative to do fun and pleasurable activities with her.

This association won't be limited to pleasurable activities themselves. Studies have shown that even while *anticipating* pleasurable feelings, people tend to like those in their physical presence more. In other words, she will even tend to like you more while *planning* that trip to the day spa together.

In practical terms, this means that before you attempt to talk about sailing away on your own boat, create as many opportunities to do what she enjoys doing, together. Plan things that give her pleasure. If that means manicures and pedicures for the two of you, so be it.

Be there

Absence doesn't really make the heart grow fonder; in fact the opposite is true. Advertisers spend billions every year reminding you that they still exist. An advertisement may not have anything in particular to tell you as in, "This program is brought to you by AT&T," but they do it nonetheless. The reason is that repeat exposure increases likeability. Research has proven time and again that the more you experience anything, the more you will like it.

Make an extra effort to simply *be there* with and for your wife. If that means skipping bowling night for a walk in the neighborhood, do it. If it means turning down the business trip so that you can spend more time around the house, do it. As long as it doesn't cause any potential resentment (she's doing housework while you watch the game), she will tend to like you more just for being around more.

From this perspective, you can see why spending all of your free time working alone on the boat is not a good way increase your influence on or likeability or get her interested in cruising. She may make jokes about you, "spending time with your mistress," but the truth is that too much time away from your wife a shortcut to unlike-ability.

Find common ground

I'm sure you may have noticed: women can be very, very stubborn. If you have already broached the subject of cruising and received some pushback, it's easy to get into a death-spiral of resentment where you each draw lines in the sand and retreat to your own corner. At this point she is focusing on how *different* you are from her. That makes you less likeable and makes her less likely to buy what you are selling or be influenced by what you are proposing.

So even before you make an attempt at selling her on your dream, focus as much energy as you can on what you share. This is where the work from the last two chapters (Ch. 2 & 3) really comes into play. The more you know about yourself and the more you know about her, the more you will be able to share.

It doesn't matter what that is: if you both like pepperoni pizza, movies, or jogging, focus on the fact that you share these common interests. The more time you do activities or share experiences that you both enjoy, the more she is going to like and trust you. This is critical to your power of influence, and critical to getting her on board.

Reciprocal affection

Straight from the psychology textbooks, *reciprocal affection* means that we tend to like the people who like us. This probably sounds stupidly obvious, but we (men especially) tend to change the way we demonstrate our affection for our wives over time. Where we used to show affection by sending flowers for no reason or kissing her on the cheek in the theater, now we clean the garage and take the recycling out to the curb. In our minds, contributing to the household is a way of showing affection, however this relaxed attitude lessens our likeability and influence.

If you've been together for a long time, go back and reconnect with what it was that you fell in love with, and focus on that. Demonstrate affection physically: hold hands and give her that kiss on the cheek goodbye. Initiate more intimate encounters, and be even more sensitive to her needs. The more you <u>show</u> her that you like her through rudimentary physical gestures, the more she is going to like you, and the more your persuasive skills will succeed. Do it for no reason, and do it without expecting her reciprocation. You'll get it anyway.

A special note on objections and reciprocal affection: you must not take any of her inevitable objections to going sailing or cruising <u>personally</u> (more on this in chapter 6). If you do take her rejection or objection personally, you may unconsciously reciprocate with lack of affection in return. This is where you go sulk silently somewhere or withhold communication. Don't do this! If (and when) she objects, just continue pouring on the charm, focusing on what you like about her, and what is attractive to you. This will be *hard, but you will win every single time.*

Make her feel good

We also tend to like those that make us feel good about ourselves. Taking a note from the last chapter, remember that she is more aesthetically inclined than you are. So yes, "that dress makes your hair look so good," is a key that unlocks the door to her heart. You do have to be genuine though. There is no need to be overt or shallow; it really just comes down to a) noticing, and b) saying something.

Get her to help you do something. Anything.

Research has shown that we tend to dislike someone who harms us (someone got paid to do this research?), and that goes for whether it was by accident or on purpose. Interestingly, the same research shows that we tend to like someone else less after *we* harm *them*, regardless of whether it was an accident or on purpose.

You may have heard the old saying, "it is the giver of gifts that gets the greatest gift." Doing favors for her is not the answer to selling her on *The Dream*; the trick instead is to get her to do things for <u>you</u>. When she does, her subconscious will tell her: *I must like this person because I am helping him*. When you notice her doing you a favor and show your appreciation for her effort, you win on every likeability front.

Smile at your own mistakes

No one likes a know-it-all blowhard. As we'll be discussing in several places in this book, it is important to act like a captain even *before* you buy a boat. What are the traits of a captain? He is confident, he knows what he is doing, and he is worthy of trust. He is a leader, but he is human. Don't let your desire to be an authoritative captain betray your humility.

Unfortunately, in trying to act like a captain, some dreamer-husbands go too far, perhaps out of overcompensation for their insecurities. Their overconfidence is perceived as arrogance, cockiness, or being condescending. Instead of building trust, they alienate.

Inhumanly perfect and confident people are not as likeable or as influential as those of us with flaws, so says research conducted by Aronson, Willerman, and Floyd (1966). According to their study, making a mistake and being able to smile or laugh at yourself makes you much more endearing and likeable.

When you show your wife that you don't take yourself so seriously, she will feel much closer to you. So when you screw up and dump the mainsail onto the deck, or ram the dock, don't ignore the fact or start cursing yourself. Instead, laugh and smile. Sailing has to remain fun, even when things go wrong.

Stay positive.

It's obvious, isn't it? We like to be around happy, positive people. We like cheery, hopeful people more; we have better rapport with them. Most importantly, positive, optimistic people are more influential and persuasive to those around them.

On the other hand, cynical, pessimistic people are no fun to be around and they certainly are less able to convince anyone of anything. It may be difficult to be Mr. Sunshine when docking doesn't go so well, your boss is being a jerk again, or the car breaks down, but it is imperative for several reasons:

1. You are asking your wife to spend a lot of time with you in a confined space. If she imagines being around someone who is unhappy or not optimistic, she is not going to attach a positive feeling to that thought.

2. You want to prove to her that you will persist without getting angry or frustrated.

3. You want to show that you are strong and confident.

4. You want her running toward cruising, not away from something else.

Avoid going negative

It has been said that, "misery loves company," and we all know how true this is. People love to commiserate, and it does form strong social bonds. However, when things are going badly for your wife for any reason, it is <u>not</u> the right time to talk about sailing *away* from it all.

I know, I know, it looks like low-hanging fruit: she comes home exhausted from work and that two hour traffic jam, and she looks like she is vulnerable to your suggestions. "Wouldn't it be great to just get away from it all?" you say, "if we went cruising, you wouldn't have to go to work and you wouldn't have that awful commute."

Her reaction in the moment may give you hope. "God, you're right," she might say, "I could go for a cold margarita and some warm sand between my toes." You smile...you're making progress, or so it seems.

Unfortunately, approaching her with *the cruising dream* as a solution to her problems will do more harm than good. Instead of creating associations in her mind between cruising and feeling good, she'll be doing the exact opposite: she'll be associating negative feelings and emotions with cruising. Counterintuitive on the surface, but proven psychology.

We don't want her (or you for that matter) running *from* anything. She shouldn't choose to go cruising because it's the least of bad alternatives, but rather because she wants to go, she is looking forward to it, and she knows it will bring you both so many positive and lasting experiences.

If you use her discontent as an opportunity to wedge your cruising dream under her lid, over time the prying may just work; she may cave in and agree to buy the boat, but she will not buy into *The Dream*. From that point on, every night of bad weather, every mechanical difficulty, every bad anchorage, and every difficult port official is an opportunity for her to compare her old lifestyle with the new, and the old will win out handily. Don't go negative!

Confidence is Key

You absolutely have to believe in what you are selling to sell it effectively, and nowhere is that more important than when you are trying to get someone to change almost every aspect of their lifestyle to join you in a fantastical adventure on the high seas. If you aren't confident that this cruising thing is going to be worth every sacrifice, every dollar spent, and all the energy required, you need to re-think your own motivations or do more research. If you still feel doubt but want to proceed, make sure she doesn't see it; you'll have to, "fake it until you can make it."

Be a decisive captain

The time to be a captain starts now, before you ever buy a boat or navigate to new waters, and that means taking a leadership position. To lead, you must inspire trust, and motivate by example. You must be confident to inspire confidence, and that is exactly what she needs to <u>see</u> from you if she is going to follow you outside of your local waters and into the great unknown.

Do your best to act with confidence in everyday decision-making. Don't hem and haw or dither around or be non-committal. Be careful not to act with arrogance or impunity, but do be a man who makes up his mind yet isn't afraid to change it if the situation changes. Depending on the existing roles and structures of your relationship, this can be fine line to walk.

Talk is cheap

You can't talk your way into a leadership position in your relationship or on a boat; you must act the part. The most effective leaders are those who don't just talk the talk, but walk the walk; they lead by example. Cruising isn't just an activity; it's a lifestyle and a commitment to a singular purpose.

Demonstrate these values in your life even before you start talking about a cruise. If you are asking her to sacrifice her house and give up her possessions to travel at jogging pace in a little boat, you may want to rethink your trip to Vegas with the boys or that big-screen TV for the den. On the other hand, if she sees you hitting the gym five days a week so that you can be in better shape for those offshore sailing classes you've been talking about, it is going to be much easier for her to imagine you in control of both your lives alone on the open ocean.

Set and achieve goals

If you have a long history of taking up hobbies but losing interest a few months later, she may very well see your latest obsession as a passing fancy. Proving that it's not is much harder when you've got a garage full of barely-used sports equipment in storage. As we've talked about before, she may not believe that you ever really intend on following through with this, "crazy sailing thing of yours," and thus your dream remains an abstraction for her. Showing her you mean business requires that you set goals and follow through. This is perfect preparation for the cruise itself.

One of the most incredible rewards of cruising is the empowerment you feel knowing that you did what you set out to do, overcoming the long list of obstacles, tests, torments, and challenges. When you return, you will have a new appreciation for your own capabilities and resourcefulness. You will also know that you can achieve anything you set your mind to.

So tell her you are going to run a marathon, then do it. Set a budgeting or savings goal, and make it. These are the things that leaders do at every opportunity. Prove to yourself and to her that you can and will do whatever it takes to make the cruising dream happen, even if you aren't yet talking about boats or routes. BE A CAPTAIN!

Find your right state

She has moods, and you do too. I was an under-slept, over-caffeinated, stressed out bundle of nerves when I first set out to convince my wife that sailing away from it all would be a good idea. The second time around, I was exercising, eating right, limiting stimulants, and even meditating. Guess which "me" was more confident and more effective?

Always in Neutral Territory

By now you've done everything you can to widen the smile on her face when you walk through the door, at least most of the time. She likes being around you. She sees that you are an optimistic and confident man who knows what he wants, goes after whatever it is, and gets it. When and where should you tell her that you want to disrupt her life for an offshore sailing adventure? The time and the place are critical to getting a favorable reaction.

When I first decided to pursue my dream of cruising, I was completely indiscriminant about where and when I brought the subject up with Megan. Often I'd pick the worst possible times and the worst possible places: I'd show her boats or boat gear in bed after a long stressful day, I'd bring the subject up while sitting in traffic, I'd talk about it while watching television, etc. Not surprising that every time I brought *The Dream* up, Megan's reaction was one of fear and anxiety.

Environment and activities

Where and *when* you approach her are just as important as *what* you say. Asking her if she wants to go sailing alone on the open ocean in a small boat while she is lying relaxed in bed at home is a little like her asking you if you'd like to become a vegetarian while you're enjoying the perfect porterhouse steak. Regardless of how positive the impact might be on your cholesterol, your cardiovascular system, your waistline, or your energy level, the vegetarian diet will never look like an appealing option as you sink your teeth into that savory carnivorous delight.

Always approach her with *the cruising dream* in <u>neutral territory</u>, when she is in an <u>aroused state</u>. Human beings are much more impressionable and much more likely to form positive impressions when in a heightened state of awareness. Don't broach the subject at home, and don't do it at a boat show. Find locations and situations where she has no pre-conceived associations, other than feeling good.

What you want more than anything in location is arousal without overwhelming sensory input. Examples of arousal activities and locations would be: a walk in the park, a vacation without the kids, a spa day, a tour of local wineries or your favorite restaurant or bar (beware that intoxication will work against you), dance night, etc. I am sure you can think of many other locations and activities where the food is good, the blood is pumping, and the stress is low.

Time of day

Remember that if she is the tentative type, there are two forces at work: your likeability and persuasive influence is working for you while her anxiety and fear of change is working against you. Her baseline anxiety and reactivity vary with time of day, so you should consider this if you suspect that she is going to be a tough sell. What time is best?

Cruising is not something to talk about over your morning cup of coffee as you rub the sleep from your eyes. Morning (6:30-9:30AM) is a time when blood pressure is spiking, testosterone secretion is at it's highest (even for her), and caffeine can add to stress hormone (such as cortisol) secretion. Her anxiety reactions can be very fast and unpredictable in the early hours of the day.

By early afternoon, her reaction times are fastest, with highest cardiovascular efficiency. By evening (after 6:30PM) blood pressure and body temperature is at its highest. By 9:30PM, the body's natural sleep hormone, melatonin kicks in, where the entire system relaxes and becomes less susceptible to stimulation (remember that arousal is what we are looking for). However, late in the day is not the best time either.

The golden window of opportunity: early afternoon through very early evening. She is alert and feeling in control, and thus least likely to feel anxious or objectionable. Beware that blood sugar considerations (see below) apply at this time since it spans the time before and after dinner.

Emotional Stability

The way she views what you've got to say will be colored by the conditions in her life that day. Psychologists now believe that 90% of all decisions are based on background emotional state, and studies have shown that emotional transference effects completely unrelated decisions. For example, if you get pulled over on your way to work for driving 28 mph in a 25 mph zone, you will be less likely to approve that raise for your deserving employee. In contrast, if you were to make the winning touchdown for your city-league flag football team, you will be more likely to buy those overpriced new golf clubs on the way home.

There are several practices and activities you can employ which will have a direct impact on her mood and thus her openness to your suggestion:

1. Control blood sugar
2. Avoid alcohol
3. Yoga and other meditative practices
4. Consider her cycle
5. Watch self-esteem
6. Sex is useful

Give up the Twinkies

Blood sugar levels are critical to mood. Insulin and blood sugar are the primary regulators of stress hormones such as cortisol, and the associated feelings of anxiety. Fear and anxiety are the last things we want her to feel at any point of *The Dream*-selling process.

Controlling dietary sugar is a fast and effective way to stabilize mood. The best tactic is to get onto a low simple-carbohydrate diet and avoid highly processed foods with hidden sugars. You'll notice a drastic difference in her highs and lows, as well as your own. As her mood becomes more stable and she feels less anxiety about her life overall, she'll be much more likely to at least let you finish your sentence when you let fly with your pitch.

No booze is good news

You might think getting her a little buzzed before you bring up *the cruising dream* makes sense, but this will work against your goal. She might appear receptive initially, but as the alcohol fades, her blood sugar drops (increasing anxiety), and the impressions you made while she was intoxicated don't form solid, lasting memories.

When intoxicated, the neural networks in her brain aren't as adept at changing and re-ordering. The result is that the next day, she won't remember why cruising was such a great idea. It's better to talk about cruising when you are both clear headed. The idea will be more, "sticky," in her brain.

Take up yoga

If you are past your peak physical condition (early 30s for many of us), I suggest that both you and your wife start some sort of exercise regimen that includes strength and conditioning training. Not only will it make your actual cruising experience that much more enjoyable, but it will contribute to a much more optimistic outlook on life and overall stabilize your moods. Just as with a low-carb diet, it may take a week or so of regular exercise before her mood is stable and predictable.

Her time of the month

I hesitate even bringing this up, but yes her cycle does matter. Every woman is different, but conventional wisdom is that for a period (pun intended) before menstruation begins and also immediately prior to ovulation, a woman's mood can be much more irritable. Do I even have to mention that these are terrible times to bring up the cruising dream? If this is news to you, don't ask your wife to go cruising.

Self esteem

We want your wife to be in a positive emotional state, but we may not want her to be overly confident. Research by Walster Hatfield (1965) has shown that she will be more attracted to you, and put more credence in what you are saying when her self-esteem has been *temporarily* injured. It would be cruel, unethical, and unfair to look for opportunities to take advantage of your wife if she is feeling down about herself, but according to this research, approaching her about giving up her career when she just got a promotion at work is going to be less effective.

Sex

It may sound obnoxiously manipulative, but one of the best times and places to talk about the cruising dream is after sex. This is a time when she is stimulated, aroused and relaxed, she feels particularly connected to you, she is riding a tide of endorphins, and she is not feeling anxious. This is an almost perfect time, provided that the sex is:

1. Satisfying to both of you (yes, you have to know for sure).
2. Not at home.
3. Not while under the influence of alcohol or drugs.
4. Does not totally exhaust her.

If she is exhausted (you're such a stud!), left unsatisfied, or if you are at home in the comfort of your king-size bed with soft pillows and comforter over top, you'll probably want to find another time.

To Summarize

What you say is just as important as how and when you say it. Keep the following guidelines in mind when you decide it's time to approach her with your dream:

1. Establish a basis for her to wanting to participate: that being her desire to be with a, "you," who is most likeable and attractive to her.

2. Only approach her with the subject in the right circumstances and at the right time.

3. She must be in a positive, stimulated emotional state to be open to your suggestions.

4. Make sure that you are in your peak emotional state as well.

The ultimate scenario?

If there were an ideal time and place, it might be after a wild afternoon of satisfying lovemaking followed by a short brisk walk and dinner at her favorite restaurant, as long as you stuck with the high-protein offerings and skip the desert and the drinks.

But what to say? How to actually make the pitch? That's where we are headed next.

5.

The Pitch

It's time to drop the bomb on her and tell her what you've got in mind. In this chapter we'll cover:

- ✓ Where many men go wrong
- ✓ What to say
- ✓ How to say it
- ✓ How to react to her reaction

Before we dive in, let's get a little perspective:

"Honey, I have an idea," your lovely wife says as you are getting ready for bed, "you know how I love flower arranging so much?" You've heard all of this before, but you'll indulge her. It's easier than brushing her off and getting the silent treatment for the rest of the night.

"Sure, dear," you say, "you really like flowww..."

She continues, oblivious to your response, "well, I was just thinking how wonderful it would be if we moved to Holland so that we could cultivate rare flowers. You know it's always been a dream of mine."

"Uhhhh……"

"Come on, this is going to be great; it will change our lives in so many meaningful ways!" Pointing at the laptop screen she says, "we could buy a little farm over here near this village on the map. I talked to a real estate agent yesterday and he showed me a farm with red flowers, and another with yellow flowers, and this other one that has a well and this one comes with a tractor!"   You force a smile.

"You could till the land and spread the manure," she goes on totally unstoppable, "I've been looking at flower farms for years; don't you think we should do it now that we've saved a little money?" You shrug.

"Come on, please!" "It will be great…" She stops for a moment when she sees that you have gone glassy-eyed. This whole speech is nothing new; she seems to bring up flower farming at every opportunity these days.

You appreciate nice flowers as much as the next man, but you have no interest in growing them.   Besides, flower pollen gives you an allergic reaction. She knows this, but goes on anyway, "it's so nice over there in Holland: no traffic, good health care, and they…" she finally stops when you don't respond. She can tell you've had enough for tonight.

You are getting a little irritated that she persists with this flower-farm badgering, but you do your best to hold your composure and give her a slightly wider, but phony smile. You think:

"Why would I want to leave everything I enjoy about my life right now? Sure, things may not be perfect, but I don't want to leave my friends and family and move to Holland. What about my job, or bowling night, or hanging out with my brother Ed, or watching the Super Bowl? And I don't want to spread manure or till the fields; I am a white-collar worker with a Masters Degree after all."

"Doesn't she consider my feelings, my needs, and my desires? She's so self-centered. Always talking about flowers, looking at flowers, trying to find a way to buy a friggin' flower farm."

"I hate flowers," you say to yourself, *"I am never, ever going to buy a fucking flower farm."*

I'm sure you see where I'm headed here, but if we want to complete the analogy for extra drama, let's assume that the flower farming is potentially dangerous, and that the flower farm is guaranteed to lose value over time. You get the point: buying a boat and sailing away is a tough sell. Therefore you must dispel all logic and appeal strictly to her emotional needs.

Wrong from the Very Start

The most common error that we men make in trying to sell our wives on anything is that we sell the way we like to be sold to, instead of the way she likes to be sold to. If you are a gear-head, you'll tend to talk a lot about equipment, features, materials, and outfitting. If you are an adrenaline junkie, you'll tend to try to sell her on the adventure and excitement and all of the new places and all of the new experiences of cruising. If you're full of wanderlust, you'll likely talk a lot about the freedom and independence that cruising affords.

The key in successfully pitching her on *the cruising dream* is to sell to *her* desires, *her* needs, and *her* emotions. She likely doesn't care how much electricity the solar panels produce, how remote and unique that destination might be, or how few marinas there are in that isolated part of the world. She is interested in the people she'll meet, the experiences she'll have, and the personal growth that you'll both achieve from those experiences.

The Moment is Here

You've done your own soul searching and done the emotional recon on her. You've taken every step possible to make sure your relationship is in tip-top condition and she likes you most of the time. You've found the right time and the right place, and the moment is here. You are ready to make the pitch. How do you proceed? Just what should you say? Just how do we go about convincing an intelligent woman to do something that will change her life in every way she knows?

1. Big picture first
2. Think global, act local
3. Make it simple
4. Be confident in your expectations of her
5. Limit options
6. Set a deadline
7. Know when to circle back

If you apply the methods in this chapter, your wife will be sold on the cruising dream and ready to take the steps necessary to make that dream a reality. Don't look at this process as a means to an end; the skills and tactics you learn now will continue to serve you well throughout the cruise.

Big Picture First

You've probably mentioned cruising or boats from time to time, but for your wife, this is at very most a concept, an idea, or an *abstraction*. At this point, she doesn't have the same imagery in her mind as you do. She doesn't share the same wanderlust that you do. She doesn't understand what is waiting *out there* for her in the way that you have already internalized. Simply sharing your interest and desires in these things is not selling. Showing her boats and destinations may pique her interest somewhat, but that alone won't get her on board.

We must offer her something that she <u>already</u> wants and desires.

So what are we going to sell?

People want what they cannot have; what is scarce or rarely available. People are passionate about things that they don't take for granted. They desire what they have to work for, and the harder they have to work for it, the more they desire it. What fits these criteria?

Time. We are going to sell her time.

If there is one thing becoming more and more scarce and appearing *less* abundant in modern life, it's time. If there's one thing that is *more* abundant than anything else aboard a cruising boat, it's time. We are going to sell your wife on time before we ever get specific about cruising, boats, itineraries, equipment lists, routes, classes, etc.

Time is the key reason I was able to get Megan on board for a second cruise, even after she said, "I am NOT going to buy another fucking boat."

The true currency of life

Time is the one inescapable and ubiquitous medium through which we all experience life. Time can never be recaptured, and it can't be bought with money. This moment, this hour, this day, this year will never come back to you with compound interest. There is no way to save time; there is no way to bank it away for a rainy day. It slips by; it passes when you aren't looking. Sadly it's only when time is gone that we begin to fully appreciate its value.

Life moves fast as we jump from one goal to another: graduation, a job, a better job, a house, another degree, a promotion, a business, a child, another child, their schools, investments, vacation, etc., etc., etc. These are all worthy goals, but we pay the price with our finite amount of time. That time will never come back to you or to your wife.

In advance of the second cruise, we talked a lot about time. We talked about my wife's goals, her growth and her needs. We talked about her father who died suddenly and too early in life (57 years old), her friend who battled breast cancer at 35 and another young friend who still struggles with thyroid cancer. We talked about not wanting to regret how we had spent this finite and limited resource on acquiring things and achieving professional status that really wasn't important in the big scheme of things. Together, we formed a basis for what we both valued most in life, and that was time.

The work/live ratio

The second time I wanted to go cruising, I knew that selling her on white sand beaches and crystal-clear blue water would never work. That tactic had already failed to deliver once. Time, on the other hand was becoming more and more precious to both of us with every year. She could see just as well as I could that we were working very hard for houses, cars, furniture, and lifestyle items that we had to have because everyone else had them.

Like many Americans, our fun time; our day-to-day recreation amounted to dinners at nice restaurants, movies, and concerts interspersed with a vacation or two every year. Life was good, but we spent about 80-90% of our waking hours working very hard to squeeze relaxation and enjoyment out of the other 10-20%. I'll call this the *live:work ratio*. For us, it was about 1:5 at best. Your ratio will of course vary, but unless you are retired, you are likely spending a lot more time working than you are playing.

This live:work ratio means very little when you are young, but as you get older, you begin to appreciate just how precious time really is. Friend's and acquaintance's lives end early or are changed forever because of accidents or disease, accomplishments fail to deliver what we'd promised ourselves, and for a variety of personal reasons we begin to take stock and question our motivations. For many, a tipping point comes at 35-45 years old when we begin to re-evaluate where all the time has gone, and what it has been used for. Some people call this a "mid-life crisis," but I prefer to call it an, "awakening."

Cruising is an opportunity to change your live:work ratio for the better and to squeeze more out of life than you ever thought possible.

Use memories

It may sound harsh, but if time seems to be passing you by too quickly, it's probably because you haven't been doing anything remarkable enough to remember. When it comes to putting value on your time, there is no better barometer than memories. If you aren't having remarkable experiences worth remembering, you are wasting your time on this earth. You will never get this time again. Ever.

Take inventory. When you recount the most important memories, what are they? The presentation you made to that client four years ago? The hours and days and months you spent watching television or going to movies? Shopping for a new car, going to the mall, or mowing the lawn? Or are your most precious and vivid memories from that single hike in Yellowstone, the visit to the Washington Monument, the dive on that wreck in the Marquesas, your first kiss, or your wedding vows at the alter? How about your wife? What memories does she flip through in her mental notebook?

Our cruising memories are the deepest, richest, and densest of our entire lives. Those are the memories emblazoned on in our minds with a depth and color that none of our jobs, houses, fancy cars, fancy meals or vacations could ever have. Even the hard times on the boat, the scary times, the rough times hold a richness and beauty that lives on brightly today.

The experiences we had *out there* live on in our day-to-day lives. We look through old pictures from the first cruise frequently. We reminisce about the people we met, and the beautiful anchorages we've shared. We retell sea stories and recount harrowing times that really could have cost us our lives or at least the boat. The fullness and vividness of those memories is confirmation of the value of those experiences, and a confirmation that time spent cruising is more valuable than any other time in our lives.

Time for personal growth and improvement

Women are nurturers by nature. They naturally aspire to take care of friends and loved ones, dedicating their conscious attention to their spouse, children, family, and circle of friends. Because they are so dedicated to the others in their lives, women frequently neglect their own needs. By their late 20s to mid 30s, your wife may be re-evaluating areas of her own life that she would like to focus on, but can't as she struggles to find the time amongst the myriad of obligations she has taken on.

Cruising will afford the opportunity to focus on herself, her needs, and her desires for self-improvement, because she'll finally have all the time in the world. Cruising is:

1. An active, physical lifestyle. After a few months of sailing, she'll find that (barring any aggravated

existing condition or injury) physical fitness improves. Just about every cruiser we met reported that they had lost weight.

2. An opportunity to relax and unwind. It's not vacation, but just about everyone we met while cruising looked healthy, relaxed, and happy.

3. A great time to develop creative and artistic hobbies. If she has wanted to write a book, improve her photography, or start painting with acrylics, cruising provides both inspiration and time to nurture her creative genius.

4. Often a time of spiritual growth and a commune with nature. Living in tune with nature and her cycles can remind us of our connection with something greater. Cruising is a time of connection with yourself and the world around you. Many cruisers report that voyaging is quite meditative, in and of itself.

Time to build the relationship

Megan and I have been together for 18 years and there is no question that cruising has galvanized our relationship and taken it to a deeper level. We are not alone; all of the cruising couples we know have expressed the same feeling of being bonded in a way that they didn't feel before leaving. I believe this happens for two reasons: time together and trust in the face of adversity.

Every boat is small, and you will find that you spend most of your time within a few feet of each other. There will brief separations as one of you takes the dingy to town while the other fixes a switch or cleans a piece of gear, but for the most part you'll do everything together. This can be a challenge at first (as we'll talk about in Ch. 9), especially for busy couples who had hardly seen each other during their lives ashore. The relationship will require adjustment on both spouse's part, but in the end, it will strengthen what you have.

Cruising will involve a thousand and one small challenges, interspersed with the occasional big problem: the anchor will drag in the middle of the night, a squall will come out of nowhere, equipment will break, etc., and you'll be forced to work together. The result is a trust and confidence in each other that will last well beyond the end of the cruise.

The storm Megan and I faced just four days into our cruise (see Appendix B) was incredibly bad luck, but we found that we worked well together when we absolutely had no choice. While the experience had many long-lasting negative impacts on the cruise, doubting each other's abilities was not one of them. After we'd licked our wounds, we found that we had a newfound respect and trust in one another's abilities and character.

When the squall passes, the sail is lashed to deck, or the anchor successfully re-sets, the sense of accomplishment is shared. It will be a team of two, you and your wife that share all of those little victories. Over time, this is incredibly powerful.

Think Global, Act Local

After you both decide and agree that time is the most valuable commodity in your life, everything changes. In the months leading up to pitching Megan on our second cruise, she and I agreed that recapturing time in our lives was our primary goal and that we wanted to increase the live:work ratio as much as we could.

To do that we agreed that we'd have to either win the lottery, or learn to live on less income. We agreed that time was more important than things, and that we were willing to scale back our living expenses in order to recapture time.

We wanted to work less and live more, and were willing to take real steps in reorganizing our life around this shift in values.

What followed were budgeting discussions, garage sales, car sales, etc. It was fun to see how much money we could save every month. We got rid of magazine subscriptions that we weren't reading, and cancelled the cable TV that we weren't watching. We didn't make dramatic changes early on, but simply slowly took our foot off the gas pedal and started to coast a bit. No talk of boats or cruising...yet.

Make it Simple

The two of you have begun to agree on a shift in your goals and values. She, like you sees the value of time over money and possessions and wants to do whatever she can squeeze more out of life. You both are taking steps to change the way you live to save more money and perhaps work less. So far you haven't talked much (if at all) about *the cruising dream* (at the very least I hope you have given it a rest for a while). So how do you go about telling her that cruising presents an opportunity to for a simpler lifestyle to increase the live:work ratio?

You must make *the cruising dream* simple and easy to understand. Again, don't underestimate how foreign a concept this sailing and cruising thing may be for your wife. Go slowly here:

1. Think step by step
2. Always provide context
3. Be specific
4. Have a plan

Step by step

If she appears to be on board with a change in lifestyle, don't get overly excited and overwhelm her by proposing an even larger change like buying a boat and sailing away. Instead, approach her with a specific plan and a very simple step-by-step process for moving forward. This plan will vary depending on your own particular situation. If you have never sailed before, your plan is going to look different than if you already own a boat and want your wife to get on board for a 9-month trip.

This book is not a cruise planning guide. If you need time to do more research on what is required to go cruising or have yet to decide on an itinerary, you should take some time for yourself, alone, before you approach your wife.

Provide context

The wind in your hair, the salt on your lips, and the freedom to choose where, when and how you go where you want to go aboard your own sailing yacht; you can see it in your mind's eye-almost reach out and touch it. You have imagery in your mind, but it's important to remember that she does not [yet]. At this very early stage of introducing her to *your dream*, she has no mental context in which to place herself. She literally cannot see herself living on a little boat visiting distant ports. You must provide this context.

References

Sales 101: Prospects demand references. Blogs, books, and magazine articles about other couples doing what you want to do are a good place to start. Forget about, "The Right Boat for Your Cruise," or, "Offshore Storm Tactics." Instead, show her the eye candy and case studies; the photos of those white sandy beaches, the deserted islands, and the stories of sundowners with friends in remote anchorages. Arouse her curiosity without trying to sell her on cruising in any way.

You'll know it is time to move onto the next stage when she starts asking questions. These can be simple questions such as, "how much does this cost?" Or her questions can be more complex as in, "how many days does it take to get from Miami to the Bahamas?"

When she asks, don't become the answer man. Instead, try to get her to research whatever the answer is with you. When she asks how far it is to the Bahamas, pull up Google Earth or other mapping program and try to figure it out together. When she asks how much it costs, pull out carefully researched articles, blogs, etc. that illustrate real life examples. Your organization will not only impress her, it will help alleviate her fear and anxiety of the "unknown."

Be specific and have a plan

Part of being an effective leader is being clear about your intentions and goals as well as what you are asking of those around you. Don't make her guess what you have in mind. This is a time to know what you want and be ready to discuss the process for making it happen. If you "hint," or come to her with a vague idea of what you want to do, three things are going to happen:

1. She will see that you are not confident and in charge.
2. She will fill in the blanks in a vague plan and find objections.
3. She will not understand her role going forward.

I made this very mistake the first time around. I was indecisive and vague about exactly what I wanted, and I portrayed this lack of confidence to her. I dropped little bombs on her here and there about how, "I want to go cruising someday." Or, "let's go look at boats." I thought I was taking baby steps to ease her into *the cruising dream*. In reality, I was waffling, being indecisive, and not showing her that I was *the man with a plan*.

For example, "honey, I've always wanted to go cruising, can we talk about buying a boat?" is vague and only hints at what you really want. Instead try, "Honey, I've given it a lot of thought, and would like to go for a three year cruise to the

South Pacific." Speak directly, clearly, and confidently. <u>Do not</u> continue with, "I'd like you to come along." Remember, we are not asking here. We are stating and looking for a reaction or objection. If she comes back with, "that is too long, but I'd consider a year," you are in business. Otherwise, see below.

What to Say

You are the captain, right? Well it's time to start acting like one. Real, genuine confidence isn't verbalized, but projected. So, instead of *asking* her to come along and participate in your dream of sailing away from it all on your own boat, specifically <u>do not ask</u>. Don't ask what she thinks about the idea, don't ask for permission, and don't ask if she is interested. Don't ask.

Convey confidence in your expectations of her

When her curiosity has been piqued sufficiently, and you have found the right time and place (see Ch. 4), it is time to say to your wife, "*hey, we could do that. It doesn't look that complicated.*" Notice that you are <u>not</u> asking for *her* permission here, and not asking if this is something *she* wants to do. You are simply stating a fact.

Her response is not particularly important at this moment in time, but be conscious and aware.

- If she responds with an objection (likely), don't address it right now-this is not bad news as I'll explain in the next chapter.

- If she responds in the affirmative with something like, "yes, we could do something like that," you do have a green light, but it is important that you not get too excited. The last thing you want to do is scare her off with the grand plan that you have waiting in your back pocket.

- If she does not respond in any way, understand that she is putting on the brakes and you should NOT continue further until it appears as though she is interested and curious. Don't take it personally. Just be patient.

Regardless of how she responds to, "*hey, we could do that. It doesn't look that complicated,*" there is no need to follow up right away. When you state instead of ask, you are telling her unconsciously: *I expect that you are going to come along with me on this.* No response is necessary.

What next?

It's likely that she will resist or object but you should not engage her in her objections at this point (see next chapter). Just keep moving forward, taking action to explore your plan where appropriate: look at boats on the Internet (in private), contact a broker and go aboard a few in your local area. Always ask her if she wants to come along. If she objects to boat shopping, tell her that you are doing research and that you are a long way from buying a boat.

Remind her along the way that she has the final say on what *she* does-you are <u>not</u> telling her what to do. You are absolutely not dominating her or creating an ultimatum situation or looking for a confrontation; you are simply acting confidently and taking specific, yet uncommitted steps toward *the cruising dream*.

If she does confront you, tell her that you are not making any decisions yet, but learning as much as you can so that you can make the right decision when the time comes. <u>This should be the truth anyway!</u>

Now is the time to learn as much as you possibly can to become a knowledgeable, trustworthy, confident captain. This will serve you well in the months and years ahead, and will not commit your wife to anything. Take a USCG safety course, become a licensed six-pack captain, take an offshore sailing course, or help deliver a couple of boats.

Not only are you taking smart steps towards competently running your own boat safely, you are proving to your wife that you are not reckless or a risk-taker having a midlife crisis. She'll instead see that you intend on becoming a competent skipper. She'll see that she can trust her life in your hands.

Limit Options

As we talked about before, we want to be as specific as possible in our cruising plans, and present that plan to her as clearly as possible. However, no one wants to feel that they don't have freedom to control their own destiny, so make sure you offer your wife *limited* options.

It has been proven time and again that by providing too many choices, you will increase the likelihood that a person will choose none of the options. Instead of telling her that you would like to go cruising for a few years, tell her you'd like to prepare for a cruise that will last anywhere between one and three seasons, depending on how much fun you are having. By limiting choices, we aren't forcing a decision, but rather removing the possibility that your wife will question whether she made the right decision after the fact. We want her to buy into *The Dream*, not the plan.

Set a Deadline

It has been said a thousand times that the hardest part of going cruising is cutting the dock lines. Your instincts are to keep on preparing, continue saving, continue improving the boat, keep on learning, all delaying the departure. At some point however, you just have to decide it's time and go. Setting a deadline makes that process much easier.

Setting a deadline for her decision to buy into *the cruising dream* is very similar. After several months of mental preparation and soft selling, you will likely have the knowledge base needed to apply what you've learned to a real cruising boat capable of going on a real cruise.

Shopping for and purchasing your cruising boat is the turning point where she must buy-in and commit. If you proceed to buy a boat without her on board, you are going to face a long and lonely road; one that will likely lead to said boat rotting in its slip. Buying the boat, if done carefully and with her full participation, is the perfect opportunity to galvanize her role and commitment to *The Dream* and make it *our dream*. Chapter 7 is dedicated to shopping for and purchasing the right boat for your (collective) cruising dream.

Know When to Circle Back

In spite of all of your hard work and thoughtful preparation, your wife may not yet be ready to pull the trigger and start shopping for the boat. If you've followed the steps in this chapter, you have done all that you can do. It can be tempting to push harder, but this will be counterproductive. Don't get frustrated or take it personally. Remember that you are asking a lot from her.

If she is not willing to buy a boat, or even look at boats, she must still have objections that we need to deal with before we go any further. To help you climb this mountain, we devote the entire next chapter to what might be stopping her from getting on board.

6.

Objections

You clarified *The Dream* in private, decided on a plan, and took all the right steps to sell her on *your dream*. She's in the right mood, you are both getting along so well together, you are in the right place and it's the right time. You say your piece, and...

Expect the best, but be ready

Your attitude plays an important role in her reaction, so it's important that you *expect* a positive response. However, no matter how much care and thought you've put into your pitch and regardless of the confidence you project, it is inevitable that somewhere in this process, she will have valid questions and objections to some or all of the idea.

While you expect a positive reaction, you should *assume* that these objections will come. Be aware that if for some reason you yourself are unsure about *the cruising dream*, she'll sense it subconsciously and her objections will multiply in response. When your confidence fails, having a response or retort ready will help her build trust in you as her captain.

Be ready.

Objections are a good sign

If you think for a moment about what you are asking her to do, and imagine yourself in her position, her trepidation won't be too surprising. The great news is that objections are a sign that she <u>is</u> considering what you are proposing. An objection is just another way of saying, "I need more information."

If she doesn't object but simply has no reaction, stop dead in your tracks. This is a sign that she is <u>not</u> curious and <u>not</u> interested. If she is ignoring you or simply not reacting to what you are proposing, it is time to step back and circle around for another try later. Her silence is a sign that you've got more work to do. See previous chapters.

Common objection themes

More likely, she will be interested in ways that she can add more time to her life and change the live:work ratio. She'll be curious about how this, "cruising thing," works, but she will have some serious misgivings about the feasibility of such a plan. Understand that most of her objections to *the cruising dream* fall into one of the following categories:

1. She imagines that this will be a <u>permanent</u> change to her life. You will meet much more resistance when she thinks this, "cruising thing," will change her lifestyle <u>forever</u>. If you haven't been clear with her about what specifically you are asking from her, she will assume that you want to steal her away for an *endless* voyage where she will never see her friends and family again.

2. She believes the decision to go cruising is a <u>critical and irreversible</u> decision, i.e. that there will be no opportunity to turn back should she change her mind

later.   If she believes there is no un-doing this decision, she is more likely to object. *The cruising dream* is a huge investment in time and money, and if she feels there is no way to turn the ship around later for any reason, or if she feels rushed or pushed, she will push right back and object to the whole idea.

3. She feels that this will be an <u>all-consuming</u> endeavor that invades every aspect of her life. She may feel that she will have to give up every aspect of her own identity to assume that of an imagined, "sea-hag." She feels she will have to become something that she feels she fundamentally is not.

4. She thinks that her <u>freedom</u> will be threatened. Without any reference or experience, she may see the boat as an island or a prison of isolation. She won't be able to come and go freely, and she won't be able to leave *The Dream* whenever she feels like it.

5. She believes that her/your <u>future</u> will be threatened. She may see the decision to sacrifice savings and earning potential as negative for your future financial position.

6. She thinks that she will <u>lose touch</u> with friends and family and lose her social status and standing.

Read between the lines.

Remember that before you can react to her objection, you'll have to decipher what she really means. She is likely saying one thing but she means something else. Here are a few examples:

- "We don't have enough money for something like this," really means, "I need to know more about how much cruising costs."

- "I don't know anything about sailing," really means,

"where and how are we going to learn how to do this?"

- "I can't live on a boat in a foreign country," really
  means, "I fear that I will never see my friends and
  family again."

You will have to use your own powers and experience as her
husband to read between the lines. No one is better at
interpreting what she really means than you. Trust your
instincts.

Responding to common objections

First of all, a response is not always required. Many times,
women are not at all interested in you solving their problem;
in fact responding could exacerbate her problem. It's
possible that she just wants you to just listen to her
objection or complaint and *acknowledge* what she is saying.
Knowing when not to respond is highly individual. When in
doubt, give her objection either a few minutes or hours, and
address it later.

Acknowledging her concern and validating it are very
important to making her receptive to your response. Dealing
directly with any of the objections above will depend on your
individual situation:

1. It is easier if she sees the cruise as finite and
    temporary. If she is concerned that one to three
    years is too long to be away, then adjust your pitch to
    make it one season. There will be plenty of time for
    you to reevaluate once you are under way. (Most
    cruising couples do this anyway. No one ever sticks to
    the, "plan," precisely.)

2. Always give her a fallback position. Don't sell the
    house and all of your possessions if she is being
    tentative. Rent and store if need be. Make sure she
    understands that if the cruise does not meet

expectations, she won't be returning alone to a storage locker and a room at her sister's.

3. Assure her that living aboard will <u>not compromise</u> all other aspects of her life. If she likes to entertain, assure her that the boat can accommodate a small dinner party. If she likes to knit, make sure she knows she'll have a place on board specifically for her crafts.

4. Let her know that she always has a <u>choice</u> and that she can leave the boat and *The Dream* any time she wants. When she feels that her freedom is threatened, remind her that she has the final say on everything she does. Also remind her that you intend to put the latest communication equipment aboard so that she will never be out of touch with loved ones.

5. Focus on how much <u>less</u> you will spend while cruising than in your life ashore. Many couples live very well on money that would be considered below the poverty line in life ashore.

6. Tell her about all of <u>social and relationship benefits</u> of living this bold and unique lifestyle. The truth is that this venture will garner her a lot more attention from friends and family than she would normally get. The people in your life will be astounded by the choice you are making. It will be a topic of conversation for years.

Allaying Fears

If she has no experience cruising, her fears may be many. These worries and concerns can be dealt with by getting instruction, experience, and knowledge in a given area. Always remember that competence = confidence = less fear. Nonetheless, cruising presents a unique set of fear-based objections. Here are the most common:

1. Safety
2. Financial security
3. Physical security
4. Isolation
5. Control issues

When talking through fear-based objections, find the right time and the right place (as we talked about in Chapter 4). She should be relaxed but aroused, and in neutral territory.

Safety

She has good reason to have respect for the ocean, as it can be a very dangerous place. So the worst possible tactic is making comparisons with life on land or explaining away her fears with statistics. I caught myself many times telling my wife it was more dangerous driving to work than sailing on the open ocean. While statistically this might correct, logic does not prevail here.

Acknowledge that her fears are valid, and tell her that you share her apprehension. Instead of dismissing her fears with comparison to the life she knows and understands, explain the classes you'll take, the equipment you'll have on board and what it is used for. Be specific.

Financial Security

The truth you should acknowledge is that most cruisers do eventually come back and re-integrate into a life ashore; very few simply set sail and never come back. Her fear (which you may share) is that you two will be left behind in the insane race to retirement. This is a legitimate concern, but the financial impact will be less than you may imagine.

Have a plan

As we've talked about, women tend to be more conservative financially than men, and it is important that you have a plan in place for that day when you do swallow the anchor and get back to work. Develop this plan together. Be specific; use spreadsheets or other budget and spending reporting software. Have a nest egg or emergency fund left over after your cruise to make sure you'll be able to transition to life ashore.

Values and habits change

We recovered financially from our first cruise within 18 months and the overall affect on our portfolio was negligible. The reason for this is that when you go cruising, you become much more frugal and conservative financially than in your previous life ashore. The habits you develop in preparation and then on the cruise itself will continue afterward.

You'll learn to simplify your life in ways you never thought possible. You are very satisfied with less, and you find new ways to save money at every turn. These financially conservative practices, habits, values and principles become a way of life. Even if you do earn less on your return, you will be very happy living on less, and you'll realize that you aren't missing a thing.

Mini-retirement and sabbatical

The entire idea of retirement is undergoing a fundamental shift right now. We will live longer and work longer than our parents and grandparents did as social welfare nets are stretched thin. Most of us won't be able to simply unplug from the working world at age 55 or 65.

But who wants to retire anyway? Statistics show that retired people are less happy, more often depressed and die earlier. Work through your most physically capable years so that you can spend your least physically capable years sitting around bored and bummed out? That's backward thinking and totally illogical.

Waiting for retirement to enjoy your life is stupid. Megan

and I both have family members who were incapacitated or died from diseases in their 50s. These were people with money in the bank and plans to enjoy it when they finally reached retirement age. Life (time) is indeed short, and possibly shorter than you expect.

Returning to work

While it might be difficult to step right back into your job or career, you may not want to anyway. Isn't that one of the reasons you want to go cruising in the first place? After returning from our first cruise, Megan and I both found jobs right away in the industries we had left. It didn't take long to realize that our hearts were even less in it than before we left. We both left those careers permanently within two years.

Something fundamental changes when you go cruising. When you return, you will feel more resourceful, confident, and capable. Starting a new career or other venture won't seem as difficult or unrealistic as it did before you left. Megan and I both started our own businesses after our short return to our original careers.

Physical Security

This can be a big one for women. Life away from the familiarity of 911, the US Coast Guard, or even being able to speak the local language removes many of the safety nets that she is accustomed to. These fears and worries are mostly unfounded and overblown by mass media.

Crime

In all the time we've spent cruising, we have only ever experienced theft on one occasion: our shoes were stolen from our dingy once in La Cruz, Mexico. The only violent crime against cruisers we've ever personally known of happened in Newport, California when a couple was attacked by American drug fiends.

Piracy happens so infrequently and is isolated to such specific geographic locations that it is hardly worth considering. Most of these crimes are against cargo vessels in well-known areas. Word travels exceptionally fast in the cruising community, and any threat is widely known. It's really very easy to stay away from the hot spots.

If she fears for her personal security, she should know that the two of you will be together almost all of the time. If she sees it as necessary, offer to take a self-defense course with her.

Health

If your wife is worried about either of your health, buy international catastrophic health insurance. While health care is surprisingly good (and less expensive than the US) in many foreign countries, there are circumstances in which evacuation to the US for critical care is a nice option to have. These policies can be written to cover the cost of both critical care and evacuation and are surprisingly affordable when you consider the wide array of eventualities that they cover. Knowing that these safety nets remain in place while you travel will take a load off of her mind.

Isolation

As a man prone to wanderlust, you may be attracted to the lonely anchorages, isolated beaches, and the absolute solitude and self-sufficiency that the cruising life affords and necessitates. Your wife has no desire to disappear forever and become one with the sea and sky. She wants to remain part of her shore-side community and maintain the relationships she has back at home. Today, staying in touch is easier and more economical than ever.

Communications

There was a time not long ago when a cruising sailboat would set off for a distant port and not have any outside communication for weeks on end. Round-trip correspondence by mail involved coordinating between ports and could take more than a month. Until a few years ago, telephone calls from remote areas cost dollars per minute. Those days are long gone.

Today, there are a myriad of radio and satellite products available to make communication from any part of the world as simple as pressing a button, and most are very affordable. We used SSB radio, satellite phones, satellite text messaging, and other tools make it so easy to talk to anyone, anytime, from anywhere. "Can you hear me now?" Yep.

A tip on satellite phones and text messaging services: rent before you buy. Most cruisers we know who use these devices find that after a few months away, they rarely use them. Lease-to-own is another great option.

Another misconception about the cruising lifestyle is that you will be aboard and away from shore most of the time. The truth is quite the opposite. Most active cruisers spend more than 90-95% of their time at anchor or in a marina where you'll have easy access (at least in populated areas) to internet cafes or other shore side internet connections. With a good connection, online videophone services like Skype make it easy to have face-to-face conversations from anywhere in the world for pennies per minute.

Plenty of new friends

It takes a special kind of person to head offshore for points unknown, and cruisers share a unique bond. The long-distance cruising community is a close-nit group of people with shared interests and goals, and friendships form fast. If you follow the typical cruising routes, you will end up seeing the same boats in harbor after harbor, and may even decide to, "buddy boat," on the longer crossings.

The people you meet *out there* don't care if you were a doctor or a garbage man ashore, or whether your picket fence is as white as your neighbors. It really doesn't matter whether you shared a couple of anchorages or buddy-boated across the Pacific, the friendships made while cruising are instant and will last a lifetime.

Control Issues

If you've been married (or in a committed relationship) for a while, you may have noticed that your wife can be a bit of a control freak at times. Aboard a small boat or prior to departure, this will manifest itself as an unending series of questions or comments that passive-aggressively suggest that you don't know what you are doing or are not competent in the task at hand:

- "Are you sure this is the right way?"
- "I don't think we'll make it before nightfall."
- "Do you think we have enough anchor rode out?"
- "You won't be able to get another job."

These are questions or comments that either have no basis in fact or for which there is no answer.

Psychology tells us that the tendency to try to control other people is the direct response to our own anxiety, so if she appears to be trying to control the situation, it is likely because she is generally anxious. It is also likely that she feels incapable and insecure about herself, not you. Her control tactics are an attempt to cover up her own perceived shortcomings.

First and foremost, it is important to *expect* that she feel anxious about setting off with you in a small boat on a big ocean. Some anxiety is perfectly natural here. Acknowledging her fear and anxiety will help somewhat as she will see that her feelings aren't a flaw, but rather a natural response. Tell her that you understand and that she is "right" to feel the way she does. Simply listening and not reacting defensively will show by example that you are in control and are being the captain.

Appeal to Her Emotions

Haven't you heard? Women are more in touch with their emotions than men. If you find that you are meeting with nothing but resistance and objections every step of the way, you may need to re-evaluate your emotional approach to *the cruising dream* to see if it conflicts with hers.

Understand her emotional logic

When you start talking about buying a boat and sailing away, it will be her emotions that determine her reactions. It's only after she feels the emotions, according to Dr. David J. Leiberman in his book *Get Anyone to do Anything*, that she'll, "then use logic to justify her actions (response)."

In other words she will react to how your proposition makes her feel before she applies any logic to what you've said. After she has reacted emotionally, she'll then respond to you by using logical arguments-that's the right, she'll use exactly what she disregarded (your logic) as she responds to how it feels to her.

Emotional priorities

You've likely experienced something like this with your wife before: you make a logical case, and her reaction is logically constructed around emotional aspects of the situation that you didn't consider. For example, you tell her she should go pick up Little Jimmy before going to the grocery store so as to miss the afternoon traffic and get home sooner.

She responds with, "Little Jimmy is always hungry after soccer practice, so I should go to the grocery store first." In this case she disregards the logic that would make for a more efficient trip, i.e. missing the afternoon traffic jam because she feels more emotionally connected to Little Jimmy's hunger than to her own desire to get home faster. You made a logical case based on your emotional needs (avoiding the frustration of afternoon traffic), but she reacted with a logical case based on her emotional needs (to satisfy Little Jimmy's hunger).

She isn't being illogical. Rather, she is responding to different emotional needs than you are.

Provide emotional framework

As men, we have trouble convincing our wives to do something because we forget to provide an emotional incentive or hook. This leaves her to create her own emotional framework, which she then reacts to. From our male perspective, this looks like she is, "jumping to her own conclusions," or "jumping the shark."

Let's say you've been talking about buying a bigger boat, and mention a great deal on a 38-foot sloop down in Trinidad. This boat is in good condition, loaded with new cruising gear, and the seller is motivated by a, "change in plans," making him willing to sell for about 60% of market value. You are excited, so you say to your wife,

> "Honey, check out this awesome deal on a Suchnsuch 38 down in Trinidad. It has an EPIRB, new sails, an oversized autopilot, and a watermaker. We could save a bundle by buying down there."

Unfortunately, your wife has no emotional framework for all of the toys on this boat. There is nothing in your list of goodies for her emotional mind to grab onto. So she says, "isn't Trinidad a long way to go for a boat? We'd have to spend $2000 just to go look at it."

It is essential that you speak directly to her emotions *before* you present logical options. A better option for the boat in Trinidad would provide an emotional framework:

> "Honey, I worry about spending too
> much money on our new boat, but we
> really need to have something more
> stable, comfortable, and secure for
> peace of mind.   We're going to have
> to travel further to find better value,
> but we'll be glad we did."

> "I found a great deal on a 38 foot
> sloop in Trinidad. The last thing we
> want is to be in a hurry or feel
> obligated, so let's make a relaxing
> mini-vacation out of it. If we end up
> finding the boat of our dreams, all the
> better."

Notice that you didn't mention any gear or even the price. By appealing to her emotionally and providing an emotional framework:

1. She knows you share her concern over finances.

2. She understands the need to find value in the new boat purchase.

3. She sees the need for a more stable boat.

4. She knows she won't feel pressure or obligation.

5. She may enjoy some relaxation regardless.

Now she's in a place where she can ask the logical questions such as, "how good a deal is it? Does it have the gear we need? Is it in good condition? Why are they selling if they could get more in Ft. Lauderdale?" These are great questions; these are logical questions that you can answer. The trick is getting her to ask the right questions and not react out of fear, anxiety or confusion.

Leverage her nurture-nature

Do you ever feel as though your wife is trying to change you? Women are sometimes accused of attempting to "fix" their men, but this is a misperception. She is actually doing her best to *nurture* and *enable* you-this is what comes naturally to her. She wants you to be happy.

Unfortunately as men, exposing our emotional vulnerability is usually the *last* thing we do. Try opening up a little; you certainly don't want to become negative or be a complainer, but allowing her to see the deeper emotions and feelings you have about boats, the ocean, and about cruising doesn't necessarily make you any less a confident captain. If you are open and honest about the personal reasons that you want to go cruising (that you discovered in Ch. 2), you will find that she will want to be a part of any solution that cruising can provide.

Additional Tips

Knowing what to say and what not to say in the moment can be difficult. If you are finding that you are bumping into the same obstacles time and again, step back, re-evaluate, and make sure that you are talking about this at the right time and in the right place. Here are a few more ideas to help move the conversation forward.

Be realistic

When you are selling your wife on *The Dream*, it can be really easy to over-sell cruising as the end-all solution to all of life's problems and the ultimate path to personal growth, achievement and enlightenment. Painting a picture of your future aboard as an endless parade of umbrella drinks at sunset and "ah-ha" moments without a balanced perspective will leave her assuming that she isn't getting the full story.

Women have an excellent bullshit detector. As you go on and on and on about boats and beaches, swaying palm trees and personal growth, she may dismiss you as a dreamer. You are, but we want her to take you seriously, so don't just talk of wine and roses. You want her to trust and respect your judgment about all things boat, and all things cruising. This requires that you stay holistic and balanced.

Provide balance by talking about the challenges you'll face. Don't scare her with storm stories or concerns over piracy, but do talk about the work required to make this whole thing happen, and be sure to let her know that it won't always be smooth sailing. Make sure she knows that you'll need her full participation.

The last thing you want to do is present unrealistic expectations of what the cruising life is really like, because even if you are able to get her on board under false pretenses, your cruising dream will not last.

Getting un-stuck

Some women have been conditioned to turn every discussion into an argument and every objection into a point of contention.   It is important to distinguish general discussion about important decisions (and there will be a lot of important decisions made in preparation for a cruise) from when she has a genuine objection to a particular course of action. When she does, you may find these methods and tactics helpful:

1. If she is not coming around to your perspective, get her moving. Go for a walk or jog, or simply get her up and make the bed. By changing her physiology, her mind and perception will change as well.

2. Provide her with new information. If she is hung up on X and Y, tell her about Z. Fresh information usually helps much more than re-hashing the same old arguments.

3. Get an outside perspective. Consult resources such as blogs, magazine articles, or best of all, other cruisers you might know. Sometimes she just won't listen to you because she doesn't see you as an authority. There is no way to talk your way into an authoritative position. We'll talk more about this in the next chapter.

4. Change your mind. If she sees that you are digging your heels in, she will do the same thing, and she will win this game every time. Instead, show her that you are willing to change your mind about something related to the objection at hand.

Use inertia

Inertia is Newton's law in physics that says that an object in motion will stay in motion while an object at rest will tend to stay at rest. The same applies to people. If you can get her moving in the right direction, for example taking a keelboat course or going for a charter, she will be much, much more likely to commit to larger sailing goals.

Called the, "front door technique," a study by Freedman and Fraser (1966) asked home owners along a busy street if they would put large signs saying "Drive Carefully," in their yards. Only 17% agreed.   Other residents along the street were asked if they would be willing to put a 3 inch, "Be a Safe Driver," sign in their window, and almost everyone agreed. Two weeks later, the residents with the small sign in their window were approached and asked if they would put the large Drive Carefully sign in their yards, and this time 76% agreed.

The conclusion is that when people take a small step towards something, they try subconsciously to maintain consistency in values by agreeing to bigger requests.

The more resistant your wife is to cruising and sailing, the lighter your push has to be and the smaller the steps should be. If you push too hard, be prepared for another physical law: equal and opposite reaction! Women can be incredibly obstinate, however once moving in a particular direction, they are much easier to keep moving.

Use inertia by getting her to commit to small steps, and you'll be surprised how easy it is to take larger ones. Captaining a charter boat in the Caribbean, buying new foul weather gear for your current boat, or maybe just taking a course together might be just what's needed to get some momentum going.

Final Thoughts

Of the hundreds of cruising couples we've met in our travels and the dozens interviewed for this book, we know of only one who decided in a single day to go cruising. She was on board from day one and they ended up sailing around the world. In every other case that we know of, it was his dream before it ever was hers, and it took time to get her on board.

Be patient

Selling our wives on *the cruising dream* is a process, and potentially a long one. It may take months or even years to get her fully on board. Continue to patiently follow the steps and guidelines in this book and you will likely succeed

It's not personal

Don't ever let t*he cruising dream* become a battle of wills. If you find that you have become adversarial over the topic of cruising vs. living ashore, you are moving too fast. You will never win this way. Instead, move slowly; deal with her objections one by one and perhaps time and again. Don't get frustrated; if you do, don't let it show.

Don't move on alone

It can be so easy to move ahead alone if she doesn't buy in right away. Resist this temptation because it will become even more difficult to sell *The Dream* once you've got the boat and the attendant "to-do" list in front of you. The marital dynamics will have changed by then and you will have missed your best opportunity for her to buy in – buying the boat. At that point, you run a high risk of becoming a "some day" solo sailor that never actually goes.

When to give up

I'll add one more piece of advice here that you may not want to hear. If you have followed the advice in this book for more than a year, and still haven't aroused her curiosity or interest; if she ignores you or dismisses you time and time again, she is not on board and may never be on board. Don't jump to this conclusion just because you are frustrated, however you may need to accept that she knows deep down in her heart and soul that living aboard a small boat and bobbing around on the ocean just isn't for her. In that case, it is best that you not try and drag her on board. In the end, she would ruin the experience for you anyway.

7.

The Boat

Purchasing a cruising boat is the turning point in *The Dream*. It is the first really substantial commitment that you and your wife will make together. This is the point at which your wife must be on board. Going any further without her buy-in is a huge mistake. In this chapter I'll share my opinions about what the "right boat" is for a tentative or hesitant wife and what gear is necessary and what is not. I'll also give you some guidelines for how to shop for the right boat.

Boat Porn

I can spend hours a day looking at boats for sale. My wife calls websites like Yachtworld.com and the classified section of sailing magazines, "boat porn." She's right of course.

Big ones, small ones, fat ones, skinny ones, those that defy explanation and description; one hull, two hulls, three hulls, I appreciate them all. I've got my fetishes for sure: carbon fiber masts keep the weight down low. I fancy the one-offs and purpose-built boats. Equipment lists tell me a story. Tonnage, beam, draft, sail area, stability, righting moment, center of effort, sheer, windage, aspect ratios...I am a connoisseur of boat design and a sailboat nut at heart.

The only thing that can satisfy my need for boat porn is the real thing, the flesh and blood: a boat of my own. Even then I have to keep a copy of the West Marine catalogue near the bed. You know, just in case.

For my wife, a boat is an object and it's an object that takes my attention away from her. As far as she is concerned, a boat is a vehicle. On both cruises, her attitude softened as she came to regard our vessels as homes, but she did not have the same visceral reaction to them that I did.

In general, women don't tend to *fall in love* with boats in the same way that men do. Where we are quickly infatuated with a boat, women tend to take their time and move a little slower. Your approach to finding a boat should take this into consideration.

Research in private

Ideally your wife will be involved in deciding what boat to buy from the very start, but as we talked about in Chapter 5, you should limit the options she must consider. Therefore, you must determine which boats fit your criteria before you involve her. Do NOT overwhelm her with 101 boats on the internet or confuse her with the unlimited choice of size, cost, and equipment list. Do that on the down-low and on your own time.

It will be tempting to ask her opinion about every boat, but much more effective to find five to ten boats that fit your criteria, print out the specs and pictures (bind them if you want extra points) and show them to her at an appropriate time.

Tips to get started

You never get a second chance to make a first impression, and this is never more true than when shopping for a boat with your wife. Aside from the guidelines in Chapter 4 for finding the right time and place, here are some additional guidelines for boat shopping with the wife:

1. Never, ever trust an online description or even photographs, and never ever bring your wife along for a first viewing of any boat. Preview all boats before she has a chance to see them.

2. Never shop at boat shows unless you can afford new. It can be tempting to try and get her psyched up by looking at the newest and the greatest, but don't unless you can realistically buy one. These brand-new gems will create unrealistically high aesthetic expectations, making every other boat look like an old junker in comparison.

3. Have a frank discussion with any yacht broker you might be dealing with before he meets your wife. Tell him that he is not to engage your wife in any way, except to answer her direct questions. I've seen brokers play one spouse off of the other to try to make a sale.

4. The law of association (again). Try and pair looking at the boat with something pleasant. It wouldn't be going too far to have her favorite music cued up on the boat's stereo system when you take her to look at it. Similarly, don't show her a boat surrounded by junkers or in a poorly maintained marina. She will tend to associate the boat with those surroundings.

5. Customization and compliments are golden. If she appears to be interested in a particular boat, tell her you like the boat but not the cushions, and that you'll need her expertise and taste to pick out the right

colors and fabrics; after all, she is so good at it! Buy-in is buy-in and if she can see herself involved in the décor or customization, you are on the right track. Give her the opportunity to make the boat her own.

6. Be even-handed in your evaluation. If you pretend not to notice the leaky headliner or the cracked Plexiglas in the dodger, she might. She is relying on your expertise to pick the right boat. Her job is to fall in love with it.

What to Buy

"Buy the biggest boat you can afford," echoed in my mind as I set off shopping for our first cruising boat, "you'll be happy to have every bit of extra space!" I read those words in a cruising magazine somewhere, and it was terrible advice. The truth is that you will find all manner of craft *out there* in distant ports with crews who have crossed thousands of miles of open ocean to reach the same spot. If bigger boats were indeed better, you'd find only big boats, but that just isn't the case.

I cannot overemphasize how <u>little</u> importance should be given to the boat in comparison to *The Dreamers* aboard her. Regardless, a properly equipped, safe craft is required standard equipment for an adventure like this. Which is the right boat? What equipment should be carried? Much has already been written about the "proper," cruising boat, and I encourage you to thoroughly research different sizes, shapes, configurations, costs, and capabilities for yourself.

It all comes down to money

After you've done all of the daydreaming and research, ultimately your market will be decided by two factors: what you can afford, and what your wife will fall in love with. It's important that you figure out the former before you engage the latter. Put together a rough budget based on your savings, budget, and timeline and be very conservative. Like remodeling a house, outfitting and readying the boat will cost more and take longer than you expect.

Recommendations

What follows are my specific cruising boat recommendations based not only on my direct experience owning and cruising two very different cruisers, but also from what I observed of dozens and dozens of other cruising couples that we've gotten to know along the way. The more resistant she is to *The Dream* or hesitant to commit, the closer you should adhere to this list. Here's what works <u>best</u> for the cruising couple:

1. Two hulls are best.
2. Smaller is better.
3. Think simplicity.
4. Lots of water.
5. Stay away from wood.
6. All boats are slow, so get comfortable.
7. Structure and quality over aesthetics, but never a junker.
8. Don't break the bank.
9. Buy something *out there*.

I'll save you the headache of finding the ultimate cruiser; it doesn't exist. Every cruising boat is a compromise and there is no ideal cruising boat; they all have tradeoffs that make one boat the best in some ways while worst in others. Everyone has an opinion, but they are all biased, except mine of course.

Get a Cat

If you can afford it, buy a catamaran. For full-time, long-distance cruising, catamarans are simply superior to monohulls and trimarans in every way. They are:

✓ Faster
✓ More stable
✓ Easier to sail
✓ More comfortable

- ✓ Brighter with open interiors
- ✓ More private, with naturally separated living quarters
- ✓ Better for entertaining
- ✓ Hold their value

Catamarans are much more like a floating apartment with a mast and sails than a traditional boat. They have large windows, with bright, open living areas, and they are much more home-like in their configuration. Instead of a "cockpit," most catamarans have more of a covered aft patio deck with a steering station or two. If you can't afford a catamaran, it is best that you never, ever take your wife aboard one, or she'll forever wonder why she has to be forced to live below-decks like the rest of us mono-hullers!

They lie flat

"Sailboats heel...that's just what they do!" You can explain the aerodynamics and fluid dynamics of monohull sailing to your wife a thousand times, but she will still feel tentative about the boat "tipping over" for a long, long time. The more the boat heels, the more she will feel anxious. I am convinced that this basic fear is responsible for most mild seasickness.

The most important reason that catamarans are better than all other configurations: they sail and moor flat. Catamarans don't heel more than a couple degrees. Psychologically, there is no inherent contradiction between the habitable living spaces (salon, galley, head, staterooms, etc.) and the "natural" orientation of those spaces with respect to gravity or the horizon like you experience sailing a monohull. This will eliminate 90% of her fear of the ocean and of sailing right off the bat.

Anchor out

In spite of everything you've read about voyaging, the truth is that you will spend the vast majority (90-95%) of your time at anchor or on a mooring. A safe anchorage is a comfortable anchorage. In a monohull, what is at one moment a comfortable, stable, flat living platform can instantly turn into a rolling (sometimes violently) barrel where dishes, books, and anything else becomes a projectile. "Comfortable" anchorage therefore means that you will have to tuck into the most crowded spots to find flat water. This will add to the stress of anchoring, and cut into your privacy.

Our first boat, *Low Pressure* was 50 feet overall with a displacement of nearly 35,000 lbs. (14,000 lb. keel). She was comfortable for a monohull, but in almost perfect anchoring conditions would often rattle our nerves. We took every measure to minimize rolling, but there were still times where we couldn't sleep well if even a small wave of the perfect frequency got boat moving. We tried everything: flopper stoppers, leaving the dingy in the water and moving deck weight down low. Every little bit helped, but even so I can't count the times I was woken up in the middle of the night wishing we had bought a catamaran.

Easy does it

Catamarans are much easier to sail than monohulls in most conditions. Sailing flat means it's easier to put that extra wrap on the winch or go on deck to fetch that loose sheet. Their deep v-section hulls tend to track well, especially with dagger boards. In all but storm conditions, sailing faster is easier as well as the boat doesn't tend to pitch and certainly doesn't roll.

Our friends Pat and Ali Schulte aboard Bumfuzzle had no sailing experience at all before they took half a day of sailing lessons on Lake Michigan (they didn't go back for the second half after lunch). They then proceeded to buy a new and untested 35 foot catamaran and sail around the world. Their story is unique and I urge you to read their blog and their book, *Bumfuzzle, Just Out Looking For Pirates* detailing all of their adventures.

If it's my ultimate boat, why haven't I ever owned a catamaran? Well, the first time around, I thought I couldn't afford one. For our second cruise, we didn't intend on being *out there* full-time; rather six months at a time, or a couple of months several times a year. That meant the boat would spend a significant time in marinas or on the hard, where storage costs for a catamaran would become prohibitive.

Cats hold their value

Every catamaran couple we know lost very little money on their boats (in comparison to what we and many others lose on our monohulls) in the two to five years that they owned them. We met one couple that actually made money on their catamaran in their two years of ownership. While the initial purchase price may be higher than a comparable size monohull, you will have a better chance recouping your investment when it comes time to sell.

A note about trimarans

I would not recommend buying a trimaran as a first cruising boat for two reasons: there are very few quality trimarans available on the market, and aside from speed and flat sailing, they offer none of the advantages that catamarans do. They are also really difficult to re-sell.

You'll find plenty of trimarans on the market that look tantalizingly affordable. There was an explosion of trimaran construction in the late 1960s to mid 1970s, but most of these boats were built from plywood and then covered in vinyl ester (fiberglass). At the time, this method of construction was deemed acceptable, but over time these builds don't stand up very well. Moisture is easily trapped in the plywood, degrading the structural integrity. A more modern and acceptable construction method involves plywood covered in epoxy mat and roving, but these boats can still suffer from rot problems.

Modern trimarans built in fiberglass or cold-molded are very popular as weekenders or club racers, but as cruising boats go they offer less living space than a comparably sized monohull. They are also much less bright, open and airy because structural members of the cross-beams and amas bisect the cabins.

Smaller is Better

There's nothing sexier than a long waterline, am I right? Those powerful sails, the big blocks and winches, the roomy cockpit; big boats are very impressive. The space inside is seductive too: tons of room to live in, store stuff, great tankage to be self-sufficient, etc. It seems counter-intuitive that a smaller boat will make for a happier wife, but this is absolutely true.

When you first begin looking at boats, all reference is to your life ashore, and a common mistake that many inexperienced cruisers make is shopping for a boat that works best as a liveaboard in their homeport. While you are living on the boat in the marina as if it were a small house, bigger is indeed better, but everything changes once you go cruising.

When you get *out there*, all that extra living space tends to fill with junk. Having more living space isn't as important as you might think because what they don't tell you in the big boat brochures is that one of the many pleasures of cruising is traveling to a new place, then getting *off* the boat. After a week or two at sea or in a remote anchorage, you will be itching for shore leave regardless of whether your boat is 30 feet or 130 feet.

Big is a pain

Big boats have several substantial drawbacks (in terms of a double-handed husband and wife crew, I'll define a "big boat" as anything over 42 feet or 20,000 lbs. displacement) over smaller boats:

1. They are more challenging to maneuver in tight spaces. This means more stress for everyone aboard.

2. They are more difficult to find and secure anchorage. You need deeper water and more swinging room, putting you further from shore and more exposed to wind and swell.

3. The loads on each piece of gear (winches, blocks, sheets, halyards, sails, anchor rode, etc.) grows exponentially with larger boats, making it more physically challenging and potentially more dangerous to operate and gear failures are potentially catastrophic.

4. Operating a bigger boat requires *more* equipment as you'll need to have mechanical advantage. You'll have to have an electric windlass, possibly powered winches, etc., to operate the boat safely. More equipment = more maintenance = more expense.

Our first boat, a Peterson 46 was fast and comfortable, but it was way too big for the two of us to handle when the wind or seas came up. When it was time to put in a reef or shorten sail, the loads on all the lines became too high for Megan to handle, so I ended up doing almost all of the sail handling. I couldn't trust her to handle the boat by herself, and she didn't like feeling powerless over the boat when I wasn't close at hand.

Low Pressure was also a lot of work to handle in anchorage and mooring situations. Again, this was not a problem at all when conditions were calm, but when the wind or current was a factor, the anchor dragged, the windlass malfunctioned, or the engine was acting unreliably, we found ourselves in a critical mess very quickly. Coming and going from marina slips was always filled with drama, with Megan falling overboard on one occasion!

The perfect size

The perfect size boat depends on your itinerary, but if you have a hesitant or resistant wife, you should always go as small as possible. For part-time cruising, pocket cruisers in the 27 to 32 foot range can provide an adequate platform for coastal hops where you expect to find abundant protected anchorage. These boats generally don't carry enough water or provisions for a couple for more than a week or so away from facilities, so you'll be confined to relatively more populated cruising grounds.

For extended cruising, you'll need something bigger. In my opinion, for a cruising couple, the best size sailboat is about 33 to 39 feet long with about 10,000 to 16,000 lbs. displacement. Any boat smaller than 33 feet and weighing less than 10,000 lbs. is going to have less than enough tankage to make extended cruising comfortable; limited fresh water will be a concern and severely affect the her comfort aboard.

On any boat over 40 feet, sail handling quickly becomes too much for your wife to safely accomplish alone and this is the key-she must be able to confidently operate the basic sail controls by herself. Electric winches, furling mainsails, and other labor-saving devices may make a bigger boat easier for her to sail, but these systems will require more expense and maintenance, taking a toll on your happiness in the long run.

Megan and I cruise for three to six months per year, and find that our Freedom 33 is more than adequate. We have just enough space for the essentials, have a reasonable range with the amount of fuel and water she'll carry, and the boat is perfectly fine for sailing on the open ocean. If we were living aboard or cruising full-time, we'd want something just a little bigger and definitely a catamaran.

Be Simple-minded

Many cruising boats become floating chandleries loaded with incredibly sophisticated gear and all manner of interdependent system capable of producing nearly home-like amenities. We fell into this trap with our first cruiser, and *Low Pressure* became symbolic of my completely misinformed priorities. This tendency to over-spend, over-complicate, and over-engineer happens for a variety of reasons, but here are the two most common:

A. Having worn her down or bullied her into buying a boat, he carries a lot of guilt. He knows intuitively that she doesn't enjoy this sailing thing, so he compensates by trying his very best to make sure his wife is as <u>comfortable</u> as possible aboard. He thinks that more amenities = more comfort.

B. He simply loves the boat like a mistress. He wants the best for the lovely lady who will carry him into the warm glowing sunset of the cruising dream. Nothing is too good for her.

Instead of investing in *The Dreamers*, these guys invest in the boat. They spend more time [and money] getting ready to go, and more time [and money] keeping the boat functioning perfectly and looking good once they are actually cruising. All the time, energy, and money spent on the boat are resources that could be used for preparing him and his wife for the trip or the cruising kitty or the nest egg instead; all things that will have a bigger effect on her comfort and happiness aboard than any piece of boat gear.

Don't dote on the boat

Our consumer culture is partly to blame here. The magazines and catalogues are seductive. They print articles on how complicated navigating or anchoring is along side ads for products that promise to solve those very same problems. The advertising copy makes it sound like you can't live without whatever it is, and the accompanying picture makes it look like everyone *out there* will have one.

Understand that adding "improvements" and oversized gear starts a chain reaction that requires other system upgrades and additions. The simple job of replacing your current windlass with a bigger one requires bigger power cables, a bigger battery to power it, then a larger alternator to charge the bigger battery. Of course you need the bigger drive belt for the bigger alternator, and you'll need to upgrade the charge regulator so you don't fry that new battery.

Pick almost any system upgrade and you will find that the rest of that system or related systems will require attention to function correctly. What at first looks like a laborsaving piece of gear ends up being a total re-engineering of the boat. There is a huge maintenance price to pay when things go wrong, and in the end that laborsaving piece of gear doesn't save much labor. In fact it costs more.

"Cruising is fixing your boat in exotic locations"

Spending the money is no fun, but time is the most regrettable cost when you have a breakdown on your cruise. Time spent on boat work feels good and productive when you are preparing for the big cruise, but by the time you are upside-down in 95 degree heat with high humidity, it's not so fun. Add the fact that everyone else is out snorkeling on the reef or getting a beer ashore, and your frustrations mount.

Both of you are stuck when things break on your boat. If you don't think rebuilding the bearing on your in-boom furler in Fiji is much fun, I guarantee your wife will enjoy you and the experience even less. While you are cursing as the tools and parts roll around on deck, she'll be thinking, "This is NOT what I signed up for."

We met a wonderful couple in Puerto Vallarta with a gorgeous boat when we were getting ready to head across the Pacific to the Marquesas. Many years our senior, they had a newer 50 footer with every imaginable upgrade, from scuba compressor to mainsail furling to electric winches to a genset. The boat was immaculate, but there was a price to pay: we literally never saw this couple outside of the marina. They spent absolutely every day working to prepare and repair all the pretty parts.

I caught up with them three years later after they had shipped their boat back from New Zealand. We talked about highlights and lowlights from their trip. The worst of times were not the Maramu storm in Tahiti or hurricane in the Sea of Cortez. Instead both agreed that the worst times were being stuck in port waiting for parts to arrive or specialists to install those parts. Their website had special pages dedicated to complaining about companies whose products had cost them weeks or even a month in port to repair.

We had fallen into the same trap ourselves. We had everything on the first cruise: scuba compressor, genset, solar panels, furling headsails, a watermaker, two refrigeration systems, and even a washer and drier. The boat was fitted out to spend months off the grid away from marinas, but that was ignorant thinking. In the one season that were *out there* cruising on Low Pressure in Mexico, all of the following <u>brand new</u> equipment required multiple repairs or replacement:

1. Windlass
2. High-output alternator
3. One of our refrigeration systems
4. One of our three fuel tanks
5. Heat exchanger
6. Engine Starter
7. Solar charge regulator
8. Watermaker
9. Scuba compressor

Adding and upgrading this equipment didn't keep us out of marinas, but did exactly the opposite! Megan didn't like me working on the boat anymore than I did. We both would've rather been at the beach or hiking or snorkeling. A simpler boat would have allowed for more time to do just that.

The joy of simplicity

We met Larry and Tenaya at Isla Partida outside of La Paz. Even younger than us, they were down from the Long Beach area aboard an older wooden schooner. They came with only the basics and a good attitude. Talk about no-frills: they had a hand-held GPS and paper charts and that was it! No autopilot or wind vane, no watermaker or radar, no outboard for their dingy, really nothing except a dry place to sleep, an icebox for the beer, and a big smile each time we saw them.

We took that to heart and adopted a simple-boat paradigm for the second cruise. Let me tell you, cruising a simple boat will reward you in so many ways: you will spend less money overall, less time and money on maintenance, have less to worry about malfunctioning, and an overall easier boat to operate day-to-day. When out cruising, you will spend your days doing fun things instead of repairs.

What You Need and What You Don't

So what exactly do you need on a cruising boat to keep your wife happy? As I mentioned before, there are plenty of resources available to help you make these decisions; I suggest that you do your own research. The following is a list of common equipment options. Where I agree, I'll describe why, and where I disagree, I'll tell you why the alternative is better.

Not essential:

1. Refrigeration. You get to have cool drinks and maybe even an ice cube or two. In reality, you will do most of your socializing with other cruisers, many of which probably have refrigeration. Trading a speared fish for

some ice is a good bargain, and a nice way to bond. Except for the longest passages on a trip around the world, you'll be able to buy enough ice just about anywhere to last a week or so in a decent icebox.

2. Genset. All small electronics can run on relatively inexpensive DC to AC inverters. Solar panels can easily supply the electricity needed on a simple cruising boat. These cost much less than a genset anyway.

3. Radar. These are helpful and provide peace of mind, but a regular watch underway will accomplish the same task. Overall not worth the expense and energy requirements.

4. Chart plotter. Nice, but not essential. When we got into hairy situations off foreign coasts, we always went back to paper charts when we had them.

5. Single Sideband radio. A SSB receiver is nice to have, but for uninterrupted and unlimited email communication, stick with a satellite phone or satellite texting device. The cost of a SSB will pay for two or three years of satellite service.

6. [Electric] Windlass. Unless you have physical disabilities and limitations, bringing up the anchor on a 36 foot boat should not require electricity. On boats under 33 feet, you probably don't need a windlass at all.

Essential

1. GPS. Just too simple and easy not to use.

2. Self-steering. Vane-type steering is absolutely essential for offshore voyaging. No crew should leave without it. A quality autopilot is nice as well (required

equipment on catamarans), but less essential than a windvane.

3. Headsail furling. Simply not a question anymore. Modern, reliable systems keep both of you off the deck when things get rough, which will inspire confidence.

4. Propane galley stove. She will end up doing the vast majority of the cooking and this is the safest fuel to use. Alcohol stoves can be dangerous and diesel is dirty.

5. Heat in cold climates. If you live anywhere north of Santa Barbara or Myrtle Beach, you'll want to have a propane or [preferable] diesel heater anytime outside of summer. A cold woman is not a happy woman.

6. Watermaker. Absolutely essential for the comfort and happiness of the wife. There is no other way to stay feeling clean, cool, and hydrated like an unlimited supply of fresh water. More on this below.

Your Wife's #1 Need

Women are tough; we are talking about humans who give berth to other humans after all. She'll be perfectly happy without all of the conveniences, especially when this is a "temporary" situation: she'll read by candle light, cook with glorified camping gear, wash laundry in a bucket and go without ice in her drink. She'll do a lot of things in the name of *The Dream* that you may not expect.

There is one thing that she will not put up with without serious sacrifice to her dignity and all that she holds as female. This one essential element is something you really shouldn't leave home without: <u>abundant [and unlimited] fresh water</u>.

Fresh water separates civilized living from glorified camping. Everything is better with fresh water. When a dip in the ocean or dingy ride to shore is followed by a quick hose-down with fresh water on the deck, the entire boat stays free of salt. Everyone on board will *smell* better, and their skin will *feel* better. The food will *taste* better. Your clothes will be cleaner. You'll drink more water and *feel* better. Nothing, and I mean nothing will improve life aboard your boat while cruising in warm climates like an abundant supply of clean, fresh drinking water.

The alternative, "getting by," with limited fresh water is totally unnecessary given modern technology. Yet in almost every cruising book I've read, our intrepid voyagers talk of rationing fresh water to a few cups per day on passage. They do dishes in salt water, and sometimes even cook with salt water. They bathe in salt water with a quick fresh-water rinse. If they haven't collected rainwater, upon reaching port they'll look for a clean source of fresh water, then jerry-jug it by dingy to the boat, which may require dozens of trips hauling a heavy load.

Make it yourself

If that doesn't sound like fun, your choice is to either have massive fresh water tanks requiring that you haul literally tons of extra weight along with you, or get a watermaker. Modern reverse-osmosis watermakers are an engineering marvel. Seawater is compressed and pushed through an extremely fine membrane that strips the salt from the H2O, leaving the purest water you've ever tasted.

The costs of these units will vary, but for the extended cruiser with a wife on board, they are standard and required equipment. Watermakers allow you to carry less water with you and use water more liberally. This will put a big smile on her face and keep it there.

Stay Away from Wood

I love the look of a classic wooden schooner gliding past with all working sails pulling. Wooden boats are works of art and I consider early naval architects to be engineering geniuses. Wooden boats are very cool, however they are universally a terrible choice for the cruising couple, unless both of you love to work on boats.

Wooden boats are romantic and can be inexpensive to purchase, but they will extract a pound of flesh to keep in working order. Boats were traditionally made of wood because that was really the only material available, but given the modern material alternatives, there is no reason to go with wood. Fiberglass really is the best option: easy to repair, extremely durable and simple to keep looking good.

She won't like wood trim

Even after fiberglass became the preferred material for small boat building in the 1960s and 1970s, builders continued to incorporate wood trim to maintain the look of the "classic" designs. I'll be the first to admit that a well varnished cap-rail or eyebrow makes any boat look fantastic. However, that piece of teak is not going to stay pretty without a lot of attention.

While you are busy taking care of the engine, the electronics, the plumbing, and a hundred other tasks that only you can take care of, responsibility for the less technical tasks, such as cleaning, buffing, polishing, sanding, painting and varnishing often fall on her shoulders. She may be on board for this the first time around, but setting her up with menial tasks is not going to make her feel good about her use of time in the long run. We'll talk more about the division of labor later on in this book.

The best practice is simply to avoid purchasing boats with exterior brightwork. Even those with fine interior finishes will become a burden over time. For those boats that do fit the bill in every other way, there are two options: let the brightwork go and settle for a natural grey look or paint over the varnish with a marine enamel with the intention of removing it later and re-varnishing when you put the boat on the market somewhere down the road.

All Boats are Slow, so Get Comfortable

Above all else, your wife needs to be comfortable aboard the boat, whether at sea, at anchor or in a marina. You might be happy enough sitting in a wet cockpit with your oil-skins and retiring to a damp sleeping bag under a leaky hatch, but these conditions will drive her right back to her life ashore. So what makes your wife comfortable aboard the boat? Keep her warm and dry (or cool and dry in the tropics), and minimize motion when possible.

Speed kills [*The Dream*]

The yacht brokers and sailing magazines talk a lot about performance. The argument goes something like this: the faster you go, the more time you'll have in port, less time underway, better chance of outrunning weather, etc. This is a valid argument; however the price you pay for speed will be comfort.

It really is the journey and not the destination that matters most, and this is good news because all boats are slow. If you really want to get there faster, take a plane. The difference between an average speed of 6 knots and an average of 5 knots is eight hours underway on a 200 mile trip. Sailing more comfortably for a slightly longer period of time is going to be much more attractive to your wife than going faster and getting there just a little earlier.

Foot on the brakes

A faster boat will perform better in light air, but in stronger winds, that speed will put a frown on your wife's face. I learned to sail on race boats, and was sure that I wanted a performer for our cruising boat. After a lot of shopping, I settled on a relatively fast yet stable cruising design: the Peterson 46. It was way too fast.

The biggest challenge we faced with *Low Pressure* (aside from Megan not being able to handle the sails) was slowing the boat down when the wind piped up. Anytime the boat was moving over 8 knots, Megan got nervous and uncomfortable. Consequently, when the wind went over 20 knots, I ended up with a reef or two, with shortened headsails as well so that we could slow down. It turned out that going faster wasn't an asset; it was a liability.

When it came time to look for our next boat, I took speed out of the equation completely. I wanted a boat that would move well in light air, but I didn't care at all if the top end was eight or nine knots with a fresh breeze. I knew that anytime conditions allowed those higher speeds, we'd be reefed down to manage a better motion. My primary concern was how well the boat handled in a seaway.

Eventually, I found the right design and the right boat. Our Freedom 33 is very stable, has unstayed carbon fiber masts that spill the wind, and sails that don't slat as hard when the boat rolls. *Either Way* weighs less than 1/3 of what our first cruising boat did, but it is much, much more comfortable. We get there a little slower, but Megan is much happier along the way.

A comfortable berth

Your wife needs a comfortable nest to be happy, and that nest is the berth in your stateroom. She will spend a surprising amount of time there, even if you have a comfortable salon. The reason is that this is where all of her personal belongings are; remember that a berth isn't just a bed.

This berth must be an inviting space where she can get away from you and the boat, and find some time for herself. A comfortable berth means good linen, a supportive mattress, but most importantly it must be warm (cool in the tropics) and <u>dry</u>. Without these things, she won't be resting and decompressing properly which will tax her attitude.

The mattress itself is very important. Many new boats come with a cheap foam mattress, and bull-nose finishes to segmented berth cushions leave a mark and are very uncomfortable to sleep on. You shouldn't skimp here. Custom coiled mattresses designed specifically for boats should incorporate space underneath so that it can "breathe," allowing moisture to escape. If you can't afford a new mattress, at least incorporate a memory-foam cover or pad. She will get better rest and be much happier for it.

Don't bring your linens from home! Cotton is very absorbent, and will make for a constantly damp and clammy berth. It is also a great material to grow mildew on if you aren't washing frequently. Goose down comforters can work well, but the ultimate cruiser's comforter is silk-filled. These are naturally mildew resistant, and offer the perfect weight for low latitudes. Sheets should be polyester-blend or silk.

Keep it dry

If you have any leak or condensation problems, it is imperative that you resolve these issues before you ever move aboard. This goes double for your stateroom. Nothing will make her more lonely for her bed at home than a leak that keeps finding its way onto a pillow or into a hanging locker.

Making sure your decks are water-tight before taking off

might seem obvious, but we found plenty of minor leaks scattered around the boat after a couple of months on board, and it was much more difficult to fix them when it involved removing soggy contents and altering interior cabinetry. We met several other crews that were also still chasing leaks months into their cruise.

Triple-check for leaks

Pressure-test your deck with a strong hose before you set off. Use a high-power nozzle and direct the stream at all possible ingress points:

- ✓ Hatches, ports and port lights
- ✓ Hardware thru-deck fittings
- ✓ Dorades and dorade boxes
- ✓ Caprail
- ✓ Eyebrow
- ✓ Hawse pipe
- ✓ Furnace vent and chimney
- ✓ Mast collar
- ✓ Stanchion bases
- ✓ Companionway

Many marine adhesives from respected companies like 3M (4200, 5200, marine silicon, etc), simply do not hold up to the rigors of topside and deck applications. The combination of flex cycling, high heat, UV, and saltwater exposure tend to make these substances brittle over time. An active cruising boat may need many thru-deck fittings re-bedded every four to five years, depending on location and load.

Cockpit protection

I hesitated writing this section thinking the topic was obvious. Then I met Morgan and Monika. They were young and just heading off for Mexico when we crossed paths in the San Juan Islands, of Washington. Morgan had spent the better part of two years bringing his older wooden boat to Bristol condition. He had done a good job; outfitted sparingly, and focused on the essentials, except for: no dodger, no bimini, and no weather cloth. Sailing in the cockpit meant that he and his girlfriend would be exposed to the weather at all times. Racers do this all of the time, but this will be completely unacceptable to your liveaboard wife.

She must be able to nest while on watch. She has to be able to wedge herself in with a book or MP3 player and not be exposed to the sun, wind, and spray. Weather cloths, which Velcro or snap into the life-lines around the cockpit add immeasurable comfort, both physically and psychologically.

Never Buy a Junker

Fixing up a crappy old boat that has "potential" is <u>not</u> the same as preparing to go cruising. Don't do it! Women take pride in the aesthetics of their possessions, so a junker is not something she will want to have anything to do with. She will not get on board.

It can be pretty tempting; I know. When you are infected with *The Dream*, you will drift off into unrealistic expectation-land pretty quick. You'll see grown men who've built companies, won precedent-setting cases, and innovated in cutting-edge industries, all scratching their chins with visions of bringing that old gal in the barn back to sea-going condition.

I know several guys who have been working on their boats for a dozen years or more. Most have spent more bringing the old hag to seagoing shape than they would have if they'd bought a new boat of the same size. They'd paid themselves less than minimum wage for years to complete the project. They didn't get a deal; they got a ball and chain.

Don't Break the Bank

Everyone comes home eventually, and your wife knows this. Instead of ignoring that fact and spending every last dollar on the boat and your living expenses, spend as little as possible on the boat. Not only does this ease her financial worry, but it allows you to be more free to enjoy the cruise, and less burdened by the boat itself.

Don't get owned

You are going cruising (at least partly) for the freedom aren't you? If that's the case, don't get tied down by an expensive boat! When we purchased *Low Pressure* and set off on *The Dream*, we sank a good portion of our net worth into the boat and her upgrades. Financially, we were just fine; but with so much tied up in the boat, we felt <u>absolutely beholden</u> to her and her complicated systems.

When this possession represents such a large portion of your total financial net worth, it will end up owning you. You will find yourself buffing out every scuff on the hull, worrying about every ding on the deck, and fighting to keep every bit of sand off the sole. There is a difference between fastidiousness and obsession, and an expensive boat will force you to explore the subtle differences - it won't be a lot of fun!

When we purchased our second cruising boat, I was looking for a capable, simple boat that Megan could handle alone confidently. The boat had to be in decent condition and not require years of work to bring into shape. I specifically did <u>not</u> want a new paint job, perfect canvas, and a spit-shine hull. I wanted a boat that could take a few scratches and dings without giving me a heart attack. I didn't want a junker, but I also didn't want a boat I'd have to worry about.

Now when we are *out there*, we enjoy the sailing, the hiking, the exploring, etc., and don't spend much time on boat work!

Buy a Boat *Out There*

There is no shame in buying someone else's abandoned dream; you'll save a ton of money by buying a boat at a downwind destination. These are the dreams that have ended, and for whatever reason, the owners have decided to call it quits and return to land for a while. Just think of it as "passing the baton" or a "changing of the guard."

Not only are these boats sometimes very well equipped and sold well below market value, but they may have already been "shaken down;" the kinks have been worked out. This saves money as well as time.

We purchased and outfitted our first cruising boat ourselves in the San Francisco Bay Area and spent almost 70% of the initial purchase price on upgrades and cruising gear. We went too far of course, but learned our lesson nonetheless.

We bought our second cruiser in Anacortes, Washington, on the doorstep to all of the best cruising grounds in the Pacific Northwest. This time the boat was simple, but almost fully outfitted. In spite of having been laid up on the hard for a year, it was in pretty good shape. The owner's "change in plans," meant that we got a fantastic deal: a 40% discount on what similar boats were selling for on the east coast.

The biggest challenge in buying someone else's abandoned dream is that there could be significant maintenance neglect. These boats are usually just buttoned up and forgotten. That last thing you want to do is buy a project boat, especially in a foreign country.

If this is your first cruising boat purchase, I highly recommend that you hire an experienced consultant to evaluate any abandoned-dream boat that you find (never use a broker's surveyor for a service like this). He or she will know whether the boat will require a couple thousand dollars and month of sanding and scrubbing, or whether you are talking about tens of thousands of dollars and a season of hiring professionals. You can save a lot of time and money by flying this consultant to a prospective boat before you invest in seeing it for yourself.

Now that You Have the Boat

You've found the perfect boat, and your wife gave the ok- now she's on board! You couldn't be more excited. You go running, tools in hand to your new prize, ready to make her perfect in every way. You've been pouring over every manual and spec sheet the seller gave you; you've got a list of things to improve, projects to complete, and new equipment to install. Let's get going! Whoa there.

Put Her first

Men love to dote on their boats, but your wife doesn't like being the, "other woman," to a collection of stainless steel, plastic, and fiberglass. She wants to know that she is your primary focus and object of affection. She wants to be the most special thing in your life.

Yes, it's totally unreasonable that she'd believe you love the boat more than her, but the evidence is right in front of her: you spend all of your spare time on the boat, you talk endlessly about the boat, and take pride in showing the boat off to your friends. (This is precisely why buying a "fixer-upper" can be such a bad idea-your wife sees that you'd rather spend time with an ugly mistress than her.)

What women want more than anything else from their husbands is to be loved and cherished. Make sure your wife knows that she is the most important thing in your life. Here are a few tips on how to keep your wife in the spotlight while you spend time on the boat:

Name the boat after her

Naming the boat after the most important woman in your life is an age-old tradition that has a basis in practical marital relations. Where and why we strayed from this practice isn't clear, but what is clear is that, "clever," boat names such as *Aquaholic*, *Ship Happens*, *Wet Dream*, or *Passing Wind* will make you look like the kid with a funny haircut and new shoes when you get to a foreign port. Being clever can get you in trouble as well. *Low Pressure* (a meteorological term related to poor weather) proved a bad idea: we ended up in a storm four days into *The Dream*. Should have gone with *Megan Julianna*.

Naming and renaming ceremonies are a fun, social way to expunge the old identity and bestow a new one, so make a party of it. Naming the boat after her and in front of all of your friends will make her blush with pride and affection.

Bring the boat alive

In the beginning, your wife doesn't see the boat as a living, breathing entity in the same way that you do. As we have talked about previously, women are nurturers; they naturally care. Why not appeal to that natural tendency by introducing *living* elements aboard?

Plants are a good option. They help clear that inevitable boat-smell, add some color to the living areas, and help to subconsciously show our wife that the boat is a hospitable space to live in. Appropriate species won't require much sunlight or attention. Good options are air purifiers like the philodendrons (the non-climbing type). False Palms (Dracaena) are another, though they will likely outgrow the space over time. The Sansevieria, also known as Mother-in-Law's Tongue (ironic name) is another nearly indestructible plant that will survive most anywhere on a boat.

Pets

We had two adorable indoor cats when we decided to go cruising the first time and moved them aboard while we prepared the boat. Megan took comfort in their company, and the feeling was mutual, until we started the engine.

The cats were fine while we were tied up at the marina, but underway they were a disaster. They peed on lines, vomited when the boat rolled, and looked generally miserable. After a few trips, they got so nervous that they began throwing up when we started the engine at the dock.

When the cats weren't happy, the wife wasn't happy. The empathetic nurturer that she is, Megan ended up focusing on the welfare of the cats instead of participating in the operation of the boat. It became obvious that they were not going to make it very far. Luckily our good friends in Portland offered to take them once they heard of our cruising plans.

On our second cruise, we had a medium-sized dog named Sugar who, like the cats had no experience on boats. While she looked a little nervous when the boat was pitching and rolling, she never got sick. We trained her to go to the bathroom on deck with a patch of green Astroturf, and rowed her to shore whenever possible.

Sugar was a pure joy to have aboard, and she provided the perfect outlet for Megan's need to nurture. Whenever it was stressful onboard, Sugar was always there to love and dote on. The dog's needs gave us something else to focus on aside from each other and the boat.

Let her make her mark

Women have an inborn nesting instinct. Even if she doesn't say so, she'll want to make the boat more homey and comfortable with her own touch. This can be a challenge because unlike your home ashore, painting the walls blue or putting up patterned wallpaper will challenge your idea of all things nautical; most attempts at home-like decorating don't work out very well on a boat.

There are several modifications she can undertake that will not affect the resale value of the boat, but add a nice, warm, personal touch:

1. Throw rugs are disposable and very useful for catching sand and other dirt coming in from on deck.

2. Monogrammed anything. Towels, sea bags, polo shirts, hats, etc. Anything that allows your wife to brand the boat herself will multiply her buy-in to the boat and *The Dream*. If you've named the boat after her, even better.

3. Pillows, cushions and soft blankets. If she can make these herself, even better.

4. Photographs. Framed photos should be screwed into bulkheads and other cabinetry or furniture. I attempted to use double-sided tape on one occasion and just about lost an eye when it fell onto the settee where I was reading.

5. Galley equipment. You'll want to skip the glass pottery in favor of plastic. Let her do the outfitting.

6. Canvas work. Having just the right thing: chapstick, sunscreen, sunglasses, keys, wrenches within reach at all times is much easier when you have small bags in just the right spots.

When your wife shows interest in adding her touch and customizing some aspect of the boat, let the project become hers and hers alone. If she asks your opinion, be honest, but always defer to her judgment. The results might not always be exactly what you would have chosen, but encouraging your wife to buy into and own the project is your goal.

Organize together

But let her lead. Organizing the boat begins the day you bring anything on board, and really never ends. Finding a place for every piece of equipment, clothing, books, food, drink, etc. is an ongoing and monumental task. Most wives are more organized than their husbands (I once asked Megan where my sunglasses were while I was wearing them), and it will be tempting to simply assign her the task of organizing the stores and spares. Don't do this; it's not fair to her and will make for headaches and arguments later on in the cruise when this or that can't be located.

Organizing the boat is a <u>team</u> effort. Both of you need to know where each particular category of thing is kept. Have her design the organizational plan for the boat. Be as detailed as possible in separating the wine from the canned goods, the filters from the belts, or whatever the case may be. Give your input, but let her own the project.

After she has designed the organizational system for storage, it helps if you work *together* to actually put everything in its place. Working side-by-side, each of you get a chance to see where this or that is kept. Later, if an item can't be located, there will be no one to blame. This is also a good time to document everything in a spreadsheet.

Simplify before moving on

Your wife wants a clean, organized space. She likes to know where things are, and have what she needs within reach. This is a challenge on any boat, but especially difficult when she's new to cruising and both of you aren't exactly sure what needs to move on board with you.

Megan and I actually moved aboard <u>twice</u> the first time. On the first attempt, we sold the house and spent about a week moving our possessions either on board or into storage. We tried our best to discriminate, but after two months of trying to live amongst and organize about 400% too much clothing, tools, crafts, materials, parts, gear, etc., we decided to move off and try again.

We rented a small cabin in the Oakland hills where we could live while we got the boat organized in a somewhat reasonable way. It took us two more months before we had everything figured out. Even then, we continued to take things off the boat over the following two years.

Almost everyone packs way too much on board in the beginning. Unless you are preparing for the apocalypse, this is a stressful mistake. Save yourself the aggravation by moving on board slowly and give yourself a period of at least a month or two to bring only what you absolutely need on board, while finding spots for everything else ashore. Remember that you can buy almost anything you need in many foreign ports.

Congratulations!

Buying, then moving aboard your cruising boat is an exhilarating experience, and a turning point; *The Dream* is finally coming alive! If simply living aboard a boat is your idea of *The Dream*, you can stop reading here-you've met your goal.

For most of us, *The Dream* means <u>going,</u> and to do that you have to actually cut the dock lines. Many couples never take this critical next step. These are the dreams that falter with plans to get away from the dock, "some day." The remainder of this book is filled with information to help you take that next step and actually GO.

8.

The Learning Curve

You've got the boat now, and your wife is happy with the choice. You've got your priorities straight: wife first, boat second. She's adding her touch to the living areas, simplifying, getting organized, and starting to settle in. There's a lot to learn about working together to make this dream a reality, so in this chapter we're going to talk about:

- ✓ New roles on board
- ✓ Pink and Blue jobs
- ✓ Giving her the helm
- ✓ Being a good husband-captain
- ✓ Motivating her to participate
- ✓ Decision-making
- ✓ Problem solving
- ✓ Teaching her to sail

Cutting the cord

You've worked so hard to get to this point to make sure she is on board with *The Dream*, and it feels like you are just about there...and you are, as long as you don't leave the dock.

When that transmission goes into gear and those lines come off the cleats, it's a whole new ballgame. In an instant, your comfortable dockside condominium becomes an un-tethered and unwieldy vehicle that requires your full attention and expertise to control safely. This thing is heavy and carries a lot of momentum; it doesn't respond quickly to throttle or helm, and there are shiny, expensive, sharp things all around, just waiting for an insurance claim.

You've probably seen something like this play out a few times at your local marina:

Husband and wife come powering in at 5 knots, he straining to look forward from either side of the cockpit with a death-grip on the wheel and throttle, she on the foredeck with a line hanging limply at her side. As they approach their berth, he swings the wheel over wildly and slams the boat into reverse. The engine whines under load.

"Honey, can you get that line...no the other one...yes, the blue one. Faster though, please, honey we're drifffff..."

"Are you sure? The one on the right?"

"Yes, do it... oh shit...NOW!!!!!!!!"

"God dam it!" "Honey, get the..."

"You said..."

"I know, but then the wind changed..."

After the lines are cleated, the damage cleaned up and the engine shut down, they avoid eye contact, as do the rest of us nearby on the dock. If they are talking at all, there isn't much smiling or any high-fives. They may bicker through their errors once or twice while putting the boat away, or maybe they say nothing. Another relaxing day on the bay is finishing on a not-so-high note. This is supposed to be fun, right?

For the husband, it's all about *getting the experience*. He recovers a few minutes later and vows to do better next time; to plan further ahead and to communicate better. "I won't make that mistake again," he says to himself.

The wife doesn't bounce back as quickly or as easily. She leaves the marina feeling hurt, incompetent, underappreciated, and out of control. She blames him for not knowing how to pilot the boat properly and loses respect for his ability and authority; she doesn't trust him as captain. She is not going to put up with this situation for very long. If "he" doesn't get better at this, she'll do one of two things:

a. Become a passenger, participating only in ways that avoid any responsibility **or**,
b. Not participate at all by staying at home while he goes down to the dock for some, "boat time."

Either way, she is not on board and *The Dream* is not moving forward.

Learn to work together

Failing to learn to work together with your wife is where too many hopeful and committed dreams end in a tangled web of hurt feelings, frustration, anger and resentment. The reasons are always the same: poor or non-existent leadership on your part, poor communication between the two of you and her lack of responsibility and participation. This chapter holds the key to understanding why you see all of those pretty boats bobbing unattended in their slips on a perfectly fine sailing day, and will show you how to avoid the common pitfalls.

New Roles

One of the biggest challenges you will face in getting your wife fully on board with *The Dream* is fostering an atmosphere where she can take responsibility not only for the decision to go sailing, but for her own full participation as an equal partner in running the boat. Be ready to make big adjustments to your relationship on board the boat, but don't forget that you share the same berth.

Pink and Blue jobs

Most couples find that they naturally tend to gravitate to more "traditional" gender roles where the husband/captain takes on the "manly" duties; the dirty jobs, while she assumes the more domestic tasks. There is absolutely no reason that egos need to get hurt over this delineation of duties on board. While your operational roles may become more traditional, your relationship and values can remain the same as they ever were.

The best approach here is no approach; there is no need to label these jobs, "pink," and, "blue," or, "his," and, "hers." As long as you both acknowledge that there hasn't been any shift in the <u>power structure</u> of the relationship-both of you are still equal partners.

If she takes issue, invite her to participate in some of your *blue* tasks. Show her to how to check and tighten the alternator belt, change the cooling impeller, check the oil, or raise the dingy on the davits. She may take to these tasks, but more often than not, she'll happily defer to you while she gets lunch ready or folds laundry.

Show appreciation

Even simple domestic tasks like doing the laundry are complicated and involved affairs aboard a boat. Cooking any more than a one-pot dish is much more time-consuming in a galley than in your kitchen at home. Show appreciation for everything that she does on aboard. Just because her knuckles don't get as bruised or bloodied, doesn't mean that her contributions aren't as valuable as yours.

Offer to switch periodically

Don't stick your wife will all of the galley duties or domestic chores. Offer to cook, do dishes, fold laundry, etc. Just as in life ashore, whether she takes you up on the offer or not, you'll score major points.

Give Her the Helm

While many job delineations aboard a boat naturally evolve along gender lines, don't get trapped into thinking that you should be at the controls at all times. Giving her the helm is a fantastic way to build trust and put responsibility squarely on her shoulders. For maneuvers like docking, it also makes a ton of practical sense.

Coming and going from the slip is one of the most stress-inducing maneuvers for a double-handed crew. The boat's speed and maneuverability are small in comparison to outside forces such as current or wind, yet even a small cruising boat has tremendous momentum due to its heavy weight, making any and all contact with other objects potentially damaging. Docking is also where you are likely to find the biggest audience and the greatest opportunity for embarrassment.

There are two key roles for a double-handed crew when departing or arriving at moorage: line/anchor handler and helmsman. Most men feel that they are the most competent with the wheel and throttle and assume the helm, while giving instruction to their wife on the foredeck. If she isn't confident or he is overly controlling, he'll give her orders about which line to handle and when and where to jump off and cleat it. This arrangement neglects two fundamental truths about men and women's greatest strengths:

1. She may in fact be better at using more finesse at the helm to control the boat and,

2. He is likely much stronger physically: able to jump farther, and better fend off the dock or other boats.

If you are having difficulty working together while docking or anchoring, try switching roles. Instead of handling the driving yourself, give her the helm while you handle the heavy deck work. Since she likely doesn't have much experience at the helm it's important that she either receive instruction from another captain and/or practice handling the boat at low speeds in open water to get a feel for the boat's maneuverability.

Control away from the helm

The person at the helm is not automatically the person in charge of the boat, and as captain, you must make it clear who is calling the shots and when. When passing the helm from one person to the other, make sure you or she say, "You have the helm," so that there is no confusion.

When coming and going from the dock, the helmsman is in control and should give orders to the deck hand, who in turn can give direction or call out obstacles. When she is at the helm you are still captain, but don't attempt to control or micro-manage; you may distract more than assist. In contrast, when coming or going from a mooring or raising or lowering the anchor, control and authority must come from the person closest to the action. This means that the helmsperson takes direction from the person on deck.

Use hand signals

Yelling back and forth in front of other boats is both embarrassing and totally unnecessary. Megan and I tried radios and radio headsets on our first boat, but found that they were difficult to hear, and make you look like a total dork. Hand signals are the best alternative. Agree on them well in advance and don't change them along the way.

Sail handling

Handling the sails is as much a part of sailing as seeing over the dashboard is to steering a car. Both of you should be completely proficient in handling the sails from the cockpit and on deck. Too many times she'll be told to, "hold the wheel," while he does the all of the deck work. The problem with this is two-fold: she is not going to feel confident handling the boat when you are off-watch or in an emergency, and she will never be able to turn the boat around and retrieve you should you ever fall overboard.

Take turns with each maneuver and sail adjustment. While as captain you will be calling all the shots, make sure to remind her that she can make any sail adjustment or trim whenever she feels it is necessary; she shouldn't wait for your command or instruction.

Be the Captain

The, "captain," is a legal definition used to distinguish who is legally responsible for the operation of the boat. Your wife needs more than a legally responsible party; she needs you to make confident and trustworthy decisions. She needs a leader who can help her conquer her fears and anxieties.

Forget "Chain of command"

As co-owners, you each have equal say in what happens with the boat. Yes, one of you needs to have ultimate responsibility and authority over the operation of the boat and the safety of all aboard, and yes, that person is likely you, the man. However, the main purpose of you "being the captain," is not to elicit obedience from your wife, but to instill trust. When she trusts, obedience won't even be a question.

You don't have to be an expert

There is a big difference between leadership and expertise aboard a boat. Let's get this out of the way from the beginning: you do **not** have to be an expert in every facet of sailing and seamanship before you depart for the big cruise. If you did, nobody would ever cut the dock lines and go. The truth is that you will learn everything you need to know by getting *out there* and doing it. The learning will never end.

You'll get contradictory advice from the "experts" who are trying to sell you their products. Cruising books, magazine articles, armchair sailors, and cruising forum trolls will give you a long list of skills to master before you buy a boat or leave the dock. According to some, before you head off cruising you should:

- ✓ Learn to sail in a dingy first.
- ✓ Get a keelboat certification before you go anywhere.
- ✓ Take offshore liveaboard classes.
- ✓ Master diesel engine mechanics.
- ✓ Learn how to anchor on a rocky bottom.
- ✓ Know how to navigate by sextant.
- ✓ Learn all of the day and night signals for various craft.
- ✓ Deploy a life raft or a storm drogue.
- ✓ Learn Morse Code, etc, etc, etc.

You don't need to learn all of these things before you take off, but you do need to have enough skill and confidence to conquer your fears.

Our friends Pat and Ali Schulte, the Bumfuzzles (who sailed around the world after a ½ day sailing class) are a perfect example. They are unusual in this regard to be sure, but I believe there are two primary reasons why they were successful circumnavigators without any prior experience: Pat (husband) was confident that he could handle what might arise, and he didn't fear what the ocean might bring them.

More importantly I believe these two were able to set off

around the world because Ali (wife) had unwavering confidence in Pat *before* they ever set off. For her, it didn't matter that Pat didn't have all the answers; she was confident that Pat would be able to handle anything that came up. Pat was already a captain before they set off, and accepted full responsibility himself.

Most of us are not like Pat and Ali. If we have doubts about our own abilities, whether from a basic lack of self-confidence or from the myriad of outside sources, we have to take steps to decrease or eliminate these fears.

Captains don't fear, they respect

A good captain respects what the ocean is capable of, but he doesn't fear it. Being a captain does not mean being oblivious of real threats or recklessly overconfident; it means understanding risks and being able to take responsibility for the boat and lead the crew in whatever needs to be done in any situation. To do that effectively, the captain must get over any basic lack of confidence he /she might have in his/her own abilities. If you have basic fears and insecurities, the only way forward is getting knowledge and experience.

If you are already confident in your ability to lead, solve problems creatively, and learn quickly as you go, then don't worry so much about having the expertise to go.

Cruising teaches one lesson over and over again: that you are more capable and resourceful than you could possibly imagine. There is only one way to find out what you and your wife are capable of; hands-on experience.

When you have no other choice or option but to figure it out and deal, something interesting happens: every other problem or mental hurdle in your mind disappears. The power and creativity that these situations ignite is addicting.

Over time, you'll come to trust you instincts to know the right thing to do at the right time. <u>Cruising will teach you to have faith in yourself.</u>

Know what you don't know

Some captains fall into the trap of pretending to know everything in order to look competent and confident, but they are only fooling themselves. The truth shines through when they becoming irritable and agitated when things go wrong. A better approach is an honest assessment of our abilities.

Knowing what you don't know, being honest with your wife about it, and asking her what she needs to feel confident in you as captain shows good judgment, not incompetence. Each woman is an individual with her own tolerances and thresholds. Some wives will trust your ability to learn along the way while others will require that you have mastered every aspect before she will sign on. Either way, she is putting trust and faith in you to keep her safe. Pretending to know what you are doing when you really don't is a gamble with really bad odds. The ocean will always flush out the truth.

Knowledge is the key

For the vast majority of us, "fake it till you make it," isn't a practical option. To conquer fears and develop the confidence to be a captain, most of us need to acquire knowledge and experience. Books aren't enough; you'll have to learn by doing.

If you are not feeling confident in your abilities in any of the basic functions that a captain will have to perform:
1. Boat handling and basic seamanship
2. Coastal navigation
3. Offshore navigation
4. Engineering (diesel mechanics, electrical)

You should take steps to address these deficiencies to boost both her and your confidence and conquer any basic fears.

There are plenty of great resources geared toward increasing your proficiency aboard the boat. Aside from US Sailing or RYA sailing classes, you can get your bareboat certification, take Power Squadron classes, or even go for USCG Licensing. Offshore sailing schools are also a good way to get experience under the tutelage of experienced offshore sailors. Additionally, chartering a boat in a destination you hope to get to in your own boat can be a really good way to test skills and wet your appetite for what's to come.

Hire a pro

If fixing things on your boat doesn't come naturally, spend some time with all of those manuals and possibly take some outside classes. A fantastic alternative is to hire a professional mechanic or boat electrician to walk you through the systems on your particular vessel. Record this pro's tour and take copious notes. This person's expertise is worth more than any classroom course, especially if he is good at explaining things.

The Effective Husband-Captain

It's difficult to be the perfect husband, and being a good captain can be a challenge as well. Put the two together is a real test. How do you go about motivating her, providing the right level of leadership and guidance, and maintain a healthy spousal relationship?

Offer her challenges

Great leaders help others believe in their own abilities. As captain, part of your job is to make her feel good about herself for what she has done and help her see what she is capable of. In order to do that, you have to offer her challenges.

Don't let her assume all of the no-responsibility roles on the boat. Don't force her into anything, but do nurture any interest she shows in navigation, pilotage, etc. You will have to reciprocate by taking care of some of the *pink* tasks as well.

Motivate her

It can be very difficult to motivate your wife to take initiative and learn new things on the boat. She'll feel a good deal of performance anxiety; she won't want to mess up in front of you. When something does go wrong, she'll look to you to take over and fix it, and in doing so, won't learn how to do it herself. So how do you get her to do more on the boat? Set her up to succeed.

For anyone to become and stay motivated, they must meet success face to face. As Nancy Erley, two-time circumnavigator and founder of Tethys Offshore Sailing for Women put it, "I want them to have success at every turn. Success breeds success."

Look for, "bright spots." According to Chip Heath and Dan Heath in, authors of *Made to Stick*, you should look for areas on the boat that for whatever reason your wife is excelling at. Take whatever is making her successful at that task, and replicate it. If she shows an aptitude for managing the provisioning, have her organize the charts. When she is successful at that, have her enter and manage the waypoints in a route on the chart plotter. When she is good at that, have her manage the routes themselves, plot the course and so on.

Don't step in

As a man, you are motivated by feeling needed or when your skills are critical for solving a problem. When you see her doing something wrong, your first inclination might be to step in and take over, to solve the problem for her. Don't do this. Unless she or the boat are in critical danger or something is about to break, let her fix it herself. This is where real learning happens and where confidence is born. Don't stand in the way of her taking responsibility!

Corrections

Absolutely, positively never raise your voice or chastise her when she does something wrong. Never, ever get angry or frustrated with her. She will retreat and be less motivated to try again next time. She wants empathy. She wants to know that you understand why she did it the way she did. Be sure to pepper any criticism with, "I can see why you thought..." or, "That makes perfect sense, but here is another way..."

Give it some time

When things do go wrong and emotions rise, it is a good idea to leave some time for emotions to settle before going back for a *post-mortem*. You may want to leave a few hours for that discussion about, "what went wrong?" This will allow both of you to see the situation with more objectivity. That way you'll learn a lot more about the boat and each other.

Celebrate wins

You cannot fawn over her too much when she does something right or meets a new challenge head on. When she raises the sail or trims the jib perfectly, acknowledge and celebrate her work. Don't, "thank" her, but rather tell her, "nice work," or, "good job." "You really kicked but on ____," goes a long way.

Don't forget to love

You are sailing a boat at 7 knots, not landing the space shuttle. There is room for affection on board. Even though you are the captain and she is first mate, you must continue to treat her with kindness and tenderness. When she is quiet or dissuaded, speak softly. Give her hugs and kisses and show other affection. Remember: listen, listen, listen – women LOVE to talk.

Decision-Making

The, "loneliness of command," is total bullshit on a husband-and-wife cruising boat.   As captain, you must not set yourself apart from your crew, and this is especially true when your first mate is your wife. It is a balancing act - she doesn't want to feel she's lost her freedom and control over her own life, yet you can't afford to be burdened with discussing every little detail. So as a husband-captain, you walk a fine line: you certainly can't make every decision without her participation, yet you absolutely cannot run a boat as a democracy. One person (you) must have the final say as captain. To solve this apparent dichotomy, understand that there are two types of decisions on a cruising boat:

1. Strategic and itinerary decisions
2. Tactical and methodological decisions

Strategic and itinerary decisions

Your wife should be included in all strategic and itinerary decisions. You should ask for, and she should be comfortable giving her opinion openly about which anchorage to head to and when. She should help formulate strategic plans for things like whether to go upwind before the heavier winds develop in the afternoon. She should help decide whether or not to go to shore before nightfall. In essence, your wife should be an active participant in all decisions that affect the *destiny* of the cruise.

By sharing responsibility for the destiny of the cruise with your wife, she'll be happier. More importantly she'll have (to borrow from aviation cockpit resource management), "situational awareness;" she needs to know what's going on. When she does, she'll feel useful, proactive, and feel she has control over her life and her destiny. These are the basic tenants of happiness, regardless of whether you are cruising on a boat or living ashore.

When she doesn't have situational awareness, you are forced into, "honey-do," mode. This means that you as captain must give your wife specific instructions at all times. This can be more effort than simply handling everything yourself. Additionally, she will not be an effective part of the team in critical situations where two people are needed.

On our two cruises, we met several boats where it was clear that the wife was a reluctant passenger, having long ago ceded all control of the cruise to her husband. We met one such boat in Mazatlan. He ran the boat while she lay in her bunk watching movies. A few days after we left the harbor, word came out over the radio that this couple had lost a line overboard while leaving the breakwater, fowled the prop and steering, sending them onto the rocks. Two pangas were sunk trying to rescue them, and the boat was seized by Mexican officials in lieu of insurance. If they were running the boat together, they'd easily have been able to raise the sails and avert disaster.

Tactical and methodological decisions

The cruising sailboat can't be run as a democracy. For all tactical, methodological, and process-oriented decisions, you as captain must have the authority to say, "This is what we're going to do here." These are the decisions about how to conduct operations, carry out a series of steps to accomplish a specific task, and decide in what way the two of you will work together. These are the decisions in which responsibility is delegated and the team of two must work together well. Here are a few guidelines:

1. Have humility, not superiority. When she dissents over your decision to re-anchor in the middle of the night, don't use a father-knows-best attitude and don't engage her objection. Instead tell her that you aren't confident that you got the hook down right the first time. If she persists, tell her, "I can see how you

might see it that way, but we are going to do it my way." Then do it your way.

2. Be simple and organized. Don't set complicated duties, schedules, or a series of six steps. Be clear, concise, and direct. Tell her what is going to happen first, second and third.

3. State alternative actions before hand. Tell her to be aware that we'll do this specific *other* thing if the boat starts drifting or the sail won't come down, etc. Every coordinated effort should have a plan "B."

4. Never, ever, ever raise your voice. When you do, you are directly acknowledging that you are not in control. She will instantly lose respect and trust in you. Do it once and she'll remember forever.

5. Don't micro-manage. Make her feel valuable by giving her autonomy, not untrustworthy by managing everything she does. When you decide that you will be tying up on the starboard side, you shouldn't tell her to tie the fenders and lines on the starboard side. Let her make the right decision. When she does, recognize her for doing so.

One last word on decision-making

How much and how often should you ask for help in making a decision? The answer here is not too much and not too little. Studies by Vroom and Yetton (1973) show that the middle road is the best here: you want her to feel confident that you don't need your hand held on every decision, but she also doesn't want to feel that she's at your mercy.

Problem Solving

An undeniable truth about cruising is that things go wrong sometimes. Many of these problems will be out of your direct control: the wind comes up fast and you have too much sail up, something important breaks, the chart or guide is out of date and you accidentally navigate to the wrong spot, a ship pops up out of nowhere and you have to change course, etc. How you and your wife react and adjust will have a tremendous impact on your happiness.

Two views, one goal

Men and women approach a predicament with the same goal, but with very different considerations. For a man, the problem is an opportunity to show his competence, skill, and strength of resolve. For him, the "how" of solving the problem is not nearly as important as the quality and efficiency of the solution itself.

As a man, you see something wrong and you immediately set aside your feelings and assume authority, hone in on it with laser-like focus. When a line is wrapped on a block or something is clanking on the mast where it shouldn't be, you are thinking, "*outta my way, there's something that needs fixin' here.*" You get straight to fixing the problem.

Your wife is much more concerned with <u>how</u> a problem is solved. She is naturally very good at integrating information from disparate sources, and wants to consider all the options. She is analytical, but above all, she wants to share and discuss the problem *before* doing something about it. She appears to proceed more carefully or tentatively, but in reality she is solving the problem in a more holistic and integrated way. She sees problem-solving as a team effort.

Recent studies at Emory University found that women are much more likely to cooperate in finding a solution than men. She sees a problem as an opportunity to explore, deepen, and strengthen the relationship with the person she is solving the problem with. Get this: she wants to work <u>together</u> to solve the problem!

Is everything an emergency?

We men tend to treat all, "problems," on a cruising sailboat like an emergency. In an emergency, time is critical: *this valve has to be fixed and fixed right now! We've got to find that leak. The transmission is stuck in reverse...where is my toolbox? What is our bearing to that ship? Ok, here is our new course... Looks like the weather is changing, we gotta move!* Conflict arises when your wife doesn't see these things with the same urgency you do. Consider the following situations:

1. You are underway and feel a jolt through the hull, hear a sharp crack, and the sound of water coming in. The boat is sinking. You must abandon ship. *This is an emergency.* This problem has a solution: get the ditch bag and EPIRB and ready the life raft. There is no need for a joint solution, only action.

2. A ship appears on the horizon and the bearing doesn't change in a minute. This means a collision is possible and course correction is necessary, but you probably have minute or two at least to execute. *This is not an emergency, but time is critical.* You probably don't need to solve this problem together. You tell her what you're going to do, and you do it.

3. You are anchored in a protected bite. The cooling pump impeller has disintegrated and must be replaced or the engine will overheat. A bolt has frozen and it must come off. *This is not an emergency and time is not critical.* If you are having trouble solving the problem, invite your wife to offer some help. Involve your wife if she is interested and useful.

4. Your anchorage is open to the south. The afternoon winds shift and high clouds are moving in quickly. Instinct tells you that changing conditions are likely overnight. In your cruising guide you can see several alternative anchorages with varying amounts of protection. *This is not an emergency, or time-critical.*

This is an excellent opportunity to involve your wife in the problem solving and decision making processes.

By involving your wife, she will feel appreciated, valued, involved, empowered, and in control of her destiny. These are all basic tenants of what makes for a happy and fulfilled person, regardless of whether or not they are living on a boat.

Teaching Her to Sail

If this book is of interest to you, you likely have more experience on the water than your wife. You are the one who grew up on boats; you were mainsail trimmer on your uncle's racer, you took sailing lessons in college, etc. You may have some experience sailing solo in your local waters, or perhaps have crewed on a delivery or two. On the other hand, your wife might know how to swim and that's it.

This inequality of skills and knowledge seems easily remedied, no? You will teach her how to sail. You will show her the right knot for the job, how to bend on a sail, tack, jibe, trim, handle the helm, navigate, use the radio, operate the radar, and on and on and on. There are three problems with this approach:

1. Unrealistic expectations: you propose to teach her everything you have learned over several years of amateur sailing in the course of a few weeks or months.

2. Teaching is the ultimate test of aptitude. What if you weren't taught proper seamanship, piloting, navigation, marlinspike, etc.?

3. The teacher-pupil relationship and husband-wife dynamics are frequently incompatible.

Teaching is much harder than it looks. I had a solid sailing background and taught classes in graduate school so I felt I could teach Megan to sail. Huge mistake. She felt attacked every time I corrected her. If things went really wrong, I stepped in without allowing her to find her own way out. She gave up too easily knowing that I was ready and willing to save the day. Very little learning took place.

When you assume you can teach your wife how to sail, while at the same time learning additional skills yourself, you are stretching the bounds of what is humanly possible. Be realistic in assessing your abilities. When either of you seem to be getting frustrated, remember that there are alternatives.

Go to a professional

Sending Megan off for professional instruction would have saved us both a ton of frustration and time. For primary instruction, this is money well spent. Learning to sail from a professional instructor:

1. She will hold herself to a higher technical standard.
2. She won't air her frustrations at you.
3. You won't get frustrated with her.
4. She will learn new techniques that you don't know.
5. She'll have higher confidence in her own abilities.
6. She will ding up someone else's boat.

Professional instructors know when and where people make recurring errors. They anticipate what is about to go wrong, allow their student to fail then learn from the mistakes. Your wife will learn more and learn faster with a pro.

Personal Comfort is Key

So far you've probably spent an incredible amount of money and attention on getting the right boat and the right equipment to make the boat your own, but you can't forget the right personal equipment. This primarily means two things: dry, warm clothing, and personal safety gear. Without it, the learning curve is going to be very steep indeed. It's hard to learn to work together if you are miserable.

I learned to sail in jeans and t-shirts with shorts when appropriate, so my standards of comfort were pretty low. When it came time to equip Megan for the San Francisco Bay we had already overspent on the boat, so we went cheap on the clothing: nylon bibs and jacket with layered ski gear underneath. Megan was miserable.

Modern fabrics make all the difference to comfort. Goretex, Tyvex, and all of the other proprietary brands keep moisture away from the skin and help to insulate against the cold. A good hat and sunglasses complete the outfit. The difference is night and day for Megan.

Safety equipment is mandatory for everyone aboard a boat. Your wife must have an auto-inflate life jacket on while on deck. Not only is she more safe, but she'll feel more confidant as well. Other gear, like a personal locator beacon may add to her sense of security. When your wife is comfortable and feeling safe underway, she will be more receptive to instruction and more active on the boat in general. An active, contributing wife is a happier wife!

9.
Life Underway

Living with your wife on a small boat out cruising is a balancing act. As we talked about in the last chapter, you don't simply want obedient crew; you want an emotionally available partner on this journey of a lifetime. How do you maintain an equal partnership as adventurers, an intimate relationship as lovers, and at the same time run the boat as captain and crew?

- ✓ Keep the fire burning
- ✓ Maintaining freedom and independence
- ✓ Have an active social life
- ✓ Avoid boredom
- ✓ Manage expectations

In many ways, life underway is a lot like life ashore. Maintaining a healthy relationship can be more difficult in some ways, but much easier and much more rewarding in others. It's easy to go after this cruising thing with single-minded focus, but you should always put your relationship ahead of *The Dream* because if the relationship suffers, *The Dream* suffers too.

Keep the Fire Burning

Cruising with your wife is one of the most romantic things you could ever imagine: watching beautiful sunrises and sunsets together, strolling hand in hand on remote beaches, enjoying local cuisine, dancing under fireworks, pondering the meaning of life with the glow of the Milky Way overhead, cooking freshly speared fish on the aft deck grill; you'll find no better aphrodisiac than fresh seafood you caught yourself.

New levels of intimacy

You'll find new opportunities for intimacy, but this is a double-edge sword: forget about his and her closets and bathrooms with a king-sized bed with matching nightstands. On the boat, you'll have a locker, a cubby, a drawer and maybe two if you're lucky. You'll spend 90% of your waking hours within a few feet of each other, sharing every meal, and every other, "personal" moment.

If there were any mysteries between you two, they'll be gone pretty fast aboard a small boat. The meaning of, "privacy," will change dramatically and you'll have to completely reexamine your expectations about intimacy. Even if you're newlyweds, all of this togetherness can dull the spark just a bit, especially in the beginning.

Getting ready

During the preparation stage, you are spending lots of money – money you worked hard for and had likely saved for a long time. You are making lots of decisions – decisions that you believe will have a critical impact on the success of the cruise and that are critical to your future happiness. You may be working at a job while spending every free moment working on the boat. Time and energy for the relationship can fall overboard.

Even if you've cut your budget to the bone, leave a few dollars for movies or meals away from the boat. Schedule time for walks and hikes if you have to. Take an extra moment to pick a flower for her hair. Make sure she knows she comes first.

Too much togetherness

Boat or no boat, you are now a married couple spending an extraordinary amount of time together. In fact, depending on your shore-side schedules, you may be spending more time together in a month of cruising than you had in an entire year of life ashore. Making the transition can be tough for some couples, so if it seems like the boat is getting two feet shorter every day and starting to close in on you, be patient and relax, these are perfectly normal feelings.

Get ready for lots of naked!

Low-latitude cruising often becomes clothing-optional, especially away from crowded anchorages and populated beaches. There just isn't much need to wear clothing when it's warm and humid and a quick dip off the transom is called for every couple of hours. You might as well save drying that swimsuit anyway, right?

This can go too far for some couples, and put a damper on the passion in your relationship if you aren't careful of "bad naked." Everyone knows the difference, and I was by far the worst offender in the bad-naked category when we first went cruising.

I got into the worst trouble with, "naked boat yoga." I'll explain: even without a major problem, the engine will require regular attention to keep clean fuel and adequate oil flowing to the parts that needed it. Our engine room was compact and required a bit of contortion to check the oil or tighten the alternator belt, and inevitably I'd end up with an oil stain on my shirt or shorts from just about every engine-room encounter. At home, this is no big deal, but out on the hook, laundry is a more involved task, so every effort is made to save laundry whenever possible.

So, I did the only logical thing I could think of: I started doing engine work in the buff, or nearly nude. This, of course, is a perfect example of <u>bad naked</u>.   You have to be in pretty good shape to be able to pull off good naked while doing engine-work. I wasn't. I'm sure Megan was scarred for life.

If you're going to be naked, make it good naked. Megan seems to have a much more refined sense of good vs. bad naked, making sure to do as much of the former as she could. She even brought along some lingerie!

If your wife does get a little too comfortable with nudity, or more comfortable than you are, be very careful in your approach. Telling her that she is engaged in *bad-naked* can be the same as giving the wrong answer to, "do these jeans make my butt look big?" Instead, try this: tell her that you accidentally saw a woman on a neighbor boat in the buff and it was pretty bad looking. Hopefully she'll get the hint.

Looking good

Physical fitness improves for most couples unless there is a pre-existing medical condition or a drinking problem. Cruising is an active lifestyle with tons of walking, hiking, rowing, snorkeling, diving, spear-hunting, etc., and are available anytime to burn off a big meal and a few drinks. All of this activity will have you looking and feeling good in no time.

We men need to be extra diligent aboard as we are much more prone to letting our personal grooming, "relax." Some captains seem to want to look the part of Ahab, but your wife won't think it's as charming. While you may feel the need to grow a beard and stop trimming your nose hair, she has no desire to try the sea-hag look.

Women are much more concerned with their own aesthetic beauty than men, which is one reason we love them so much. Living on a boat presents a challenge to her ability to wear make-up, do her hair, etc. While she might not look any less desirable to you, this can have a significant affect on how she feels about herself. As silly as it might seem on a boat where every square inch is occupied by something important to the cruise, it is imperative that you not only provide dedicated space for her creams, lotions, make-up, hair products, etc, but that you *encourage* her to make use of it.

Schedule sex

Scheduling nooky with your wife? This might sound a little stupid since you are spending so much time together, but the opposite is true when you are out on passage, where usually only one of you will be on watch at any given time while the other is asleep, reading, cooking, doing maintenance, etc. When the watch changes, the other comes on deck, gets an update on weather, navigation, any sail trim, and then stands watch for the next stretch. Little intimacy is involved with any of these interactions, let alone sex.

Some long-distance voyagers have found that scheduling sex was just what was needed to bring the fire back to their relationship. We met Janna and Graeme Cawrse-Esarey in La Cruz, Mexico in 2004. They were relatively young like us, and heading in the same general direction (the South Pacific) aboard their Hallberg-Rassy 35, *Dragonfly*.

Janna swears that making a special effort to have a, "cocktail hour," complete with pretty umbrella drinks (but no alcohol) every day helped take their minds off of the tedium of passage making, and spiced up their love life as well. Further, Janna told me that they actually went so far as to schedule sex. Without making that extra effort and commitment, it just wasn't going to happen otherwise. Janna later wrote a book about her relationship with her husband called, *The Motion of the Ocean*.

Freedom and Independence

For many of us, one of the most attractive thing about going cruising is being free to do what we want, when we want. One of the biggest surprises I had when we were first out cruising was just how <u>little</u> freedom I felt. Sure, I didn't answer to anyone and could do whatever I pleased; there was no boss around to tell me what to do. However, too often I didn't exercise that freedom because of boat work, or because I didn't want to strand my wife.

Spending so much time with her, I developed what I call, "emotional codependence," with my wife. In your life ashore, you probably spend the bulk of your waking hours separate from your wife. You'll check in several times a day, but you aren't in physical proximity for most of your waking hours. When you are close to each other in the evenings and on weekends, your moods inevitably become linked; you tend affect each other emotionally: if she is in a bad mood, this can drag you down and vice versa.

Aboard a boat, you will spend most of your time together. Not only will your moods become more correlated, but you will tend to amplify each other's feelings. In this environment, small gripes can become big issues much faster. Extra diligence is required to keep each other on an even keel, especially if things aren't going well. Each of you needs a place to escape.

No-Approach Zone

You and she will find plenty of <u>time</u> to be alone when out cruising. There will be almost unlimited opportunity to curl up with your own book, write poetry, do photography or videography, etc. Finding your own physical space on the boat is more difficult, but absolutely necessary. The trick is to dedicate a predefined, "no-approach," zone. A no-approach zone is simply a personal spot (outside of your own berth) where the other is not to approach you unless you otherwise initiate an interaction.

Personal iPod / laptop

Whether on watch or off, having her own music and her own photo album, online journal or blog, etc. will help her create her own mental space and get away for a while. In the effort to minimize "stuff," and maximize space on board, you may be tempted to share. However with MP3 players the size of a postage stamp and small laptop computers, there should be room aboard even the smallest boats for a <u>his</u> and a <u>hers</u>.

In the case of laptops, it's a good idea to back up all navigational software and charts so that if one laptop were to break or get stolen, the "business," of electronic route planning and navigation can go on.

A dinghy for each

To keep from feeling trapped aboard the boat, you should have at least two ways off (aside from swimming). At least one of these should be fully operable without your help. This means that neither of you is ever stranded on board if the other decides to head into town, go fishing, get some exercise, visit another boat, etc. When you spend 24/7 with your mate, autonomy = happiness.

You do not need to have two fully equipped dinghies on board. One primary tender will do, with a second, lightweight craft. An easily stowed inflatable kayak or raft will work as a backup to give the other one of you an option should the primary be in use. Simply having the perception of freedom will do wonders for both of you, even if you don't use it very often.

Social Life

In your version of *The Dream*, your boat swings on a sturdy anchor in a deserted bay surrounded by an uninhabited beach with blue skies above. For many low-latitude cruisers, the cruising reality is much different. Aside from offshore voyages, you'll likely have more social opportunities while cruising than you ever had on terra firma. Raft-ups, beach potlucks, and good old-fashioned meeting the neighbors will fill most afternoons and evenings.

The Pack

Cruising relationships are priceless. Unlike those nice folks you met on vacation in Hawaii, you will stay friends with some of these boats (their owners and crews) for a lifetime. You'll find that your itineraries will be similar, with weather and routing concerns putting you on the same voyages and at the same destinations at the same time.

While this can be really helpful in making your wife feel less, "alone," out there, I've met several crews who got tired and burned out from hanging out with the same people in every anchorage. Part of the reason you chose this lifestyle was to meet new people and explore new places and cultures. The, "pack mentality," can put a damper on these pursuits, and smother *The Dream* a bit. Remember that your rudder is perfectly capable of steering the boat in a new direction.

Your social needs and those of your wife may vary wildly. She may want to spend a lot of time with other couples when the opportunity is there. You may prefer to explore the local town or village and spend time with the locals, or spend a more time by yourself. If you are feeling strained by her needs, or she is feeling trapped by yours, it's helpful to talk about it freely and openly. This is where two dinghies can come in really handy.

Gossip

One favorite cruiser pastime that I never anticipated was gossip. Megan didn't seem to fall into the gossip trap, but we both met plenty of cruisers with a proclivity towards, "spreading news." Unlimited time, boredom, and habits from previous lives ashore seem to breed gossip in the cruising community as bad as any soap opera. While you may not be prone to gossiping yourself, your wife *might* be. Not all women carry the gene, but if you do find that your wife carries on with judgmental, critical discussion with or about other boats in the fleet, remind her of just how small the cruising community is and how damaging it is to you <u>both</u>.

When you move aboard and go cruising, you will lose some of your individual self-identity. Instead of Joe Smith of Little Rock, you will be Joe and Mary of *Freedom Song*. In as much you and your wife will have some individual friendships; you will be viewed and addressed as a unit most of the time. So when and if your wife gossips, it's the same as you gossiping too.

Alcohol

With total freedom and unlimited time, cruising offers more opportunity to drink more than you do now. Drinking and cruising seem to go together like butt and underwear. With no rules and no oversight, most of the taboos about drinking early in the day and drinking to excess are ignored. It's not as though everyone we met would qualify as an alcoholic, but we were surprised by how much heavy drinking we saw in general. In all of our cruising experience, we have only met one dry boat.

While most people in the cruising fleet seem to be responsible drinkers, alcoholism seems to run at a higher rate that what we've seen ashore. We met a boat in Barra de Navidad where the couple seemed to be getting along just fine. A few days later, an obviously hung-over husband explained that his wife had gotten angry with him and caught a plane home. He asked if we knew anyone who wanted to crew to Panama.

We invited two friends (who didn't previously know each other) to crew on the trip from Mexico to the Marquesas. Both were intelligent, friendly, mellow guys with apparently no attitude or personality conflicts at all. To celebrate our pending departure for the South Pacific, we all drank hard one afternoon on the beach. The party continued into the evening hours, and we barely made it back to the boat. Late that night, one friend insulted the other and the argument almost became physical. We had to ask one of the crew to leave the boat, and haven't talked to him again to this day.

Problems with alcohol are very personal and individual. This book will never be able to offer counsel or guidelines about how much is too much or what to do about it if you or someone you know *out there* develops a problem. However, I do offer this advice: if you suspect that you or your wife <u>may</u> have a drinking problem (or genetic predisposition) or even if it <u>might</u> be an issue, you owe it to yourself and to her to be hyper-vigilant as you set out on this dream. A pre-departure evaluation from an addiction specialist may just save your dream, your marriage or your life.

Boredom

White sand beaches and warm, crystal clear blue waters <u>are</u> the reality of *the cruising dream*. You will be able to see every ripple in the sand 30 feet below your boat. The warm trade winds will provide just the right relief as you sit in the cockpit with a great book. The reality will live up to your fantasy. It really is that wonderful... the first time, the tenth time, the twentieth time...but eventually life in the tropics will become somewhat routine, dare I say, even boring.

As we reached the end of year one in our planned five-year cruise, things were going fairly well: we had plenty of money in the bank, a healthy nest egg to return to, and had learned to run the boat efficiently together. We were getting along just fine, and enjoying the freedom of our lifestyle. But one thing was killing our dream out from under us: <u>too much *Scrabble*</u>.

Once you are *out there*, living the life that you have sacrificed so much for to live, nothing is more dangerous to *The Dream* than boredom. An idle mind is a dangerous mind, and the cruising lifestyle presents nearly unlimited time to think.

Both Megan and I felt trapped in our own heads at times during that first cruise. After years of hard work in our careers, followed by an intense period of preparing for departure where time was always stretched thin, we got out there and had a hard time decompressing. We both found ourselves looking at our idle hands and thinking:

"Did we make a mistake here?"

"Are we just being lazy?"

"Are we adventurers or just deluded homeless people?"

"Are we losing our place in the social order?"

"Is this as good as it gets?"

These are the same questions that many retired people end up asking themselves. Expect these ideas and emotions to come and they'll lose their punch. Also, the best defense is a good offense.

Be proactive

Staying ahead of boredom is critical. Be proactive and occupy yourself outside of the boat. She needs to have her own creative projects and activities, too. This can involve any number of things from shell collecting to photography to writing, to learning languages to surfing. The important thing is to continue learning and engaging in the world around you.

Keep on movin'

The old saying, "ships and men rot in port," is absolutely true. Make sure you keep moving, exploring; maintain a curious mind and never stop learning during your cruise. When weather or mechanical difficulties keep you stuck in one place, don't let the exploration stop: get off the boat for land travel, make friends with locals, get involved. Whatever it takes!

Managing Expectations

This starts the day you pitch *The Dream*, and never stops. Selling her with pretty pictures and stories of perfect anchorages and friendly natives can be costly once you are *out there*. Reality may not live up: anchorages will sometimes be windy and uncomfortable, the water won't always be crystal clear, and officials and their requirements can be difficult, etc. It's difficult, especially on those cold nights sacrificing or preparing for the cruise, but it's better to not have unrealistic expectations.

Go with the flow

Cruisers talk about having plans, "written in sand at low tide." Instead of referring to a flexible itinerary, they really mean that they stay <u>open to whatever experience manifests itself</u>. Ideally, both of you will learn quickly that not having expectations is crucial to enjoying the experience. You'll discover that "going with the flow" is much easier than against it. This attitude carries on nicely after you are back on land.

Don't listen to experts

It is possible to know "too much" and rob yourself of the joy of discovery. Every book, magazine, or "experienced" cruiser will give you advice and opinion about where to go, how to get there, and what you'll find once you arrive. This advice and opinion can be really helpful in navigating new landfalls, but it does have a price: it creates expectations.

Setting arbitrary benchmarks about a place you read about in a book is totally unnecessary. I personally have enjoyed many places that other cruisers or the guide books have outright panned. I know of others who have enjoyed the, "most dangerous," countries more than any other. Their conclusions were that the *facts* found in guidebooks were more like opinions in disguise.

The magic of the cruising lifestyle is that you get to set your own pace and go your own way. This may take a little while to get used to. In the meantime, don't forget to remember you are free!

10.
Troubleshooting

There is a manual for just about everything on the boat, except your wife. This book falls short of a manual (writing one is impossible), but I hope I've been able to help with tips and advice to help get her on board and keep her happy on board during your cruise. This chapter deals with some more common problems you'll have with your wife; that most precious and important component on the boat and *The Dream*:

✓ Seasickness
✓ Funk
✓ Stress
✓ Moodiness
✓ Unhappiness
✓ Complaining
✓ Arguments
✓ Power Struggles

As with any troubleshooting guide, it is impossible to answer every question and deal with every contingency. These are the most common wife-related problems aboard the cruising boat.

Seasickness

Everyone is susceptible to seasickness; it's just a question of how prone you are, but it seems like women are affected more than men. Seasickness is not just unpleasant or inconvenient; it can completely incapacitate a person. On a double-handed sailboat, that can be dangerous for both of you.

Women unequally affected

Women seem to feel seasickness much more often and much more severely than men in the exact same conditions. It would appear that women might in general be more prone to seasickness, but why would this be? Is it a physical difference in tolerance? I speculate that not only are there emotional factors, but behavioral differences that make women more sick and more often.

Fear and inactivity make it worse

While not the sole reason, I believe that fear and anxiety are important factors that make one person more susceptible to seasickness than another. All things being equal, if a person has underlying fear and anxiety about the wind, waves, sounds, and heeling of the boat, they will be more likely to feel seasick. By this logic, the more experience you have at sea, the less anxiety you'll feel and the less seasickness you'll have. Typically, this is exactly what happens.

The second reason I believe that wives are more prone to seasickness is that men too often are much more active and thus distracted on board. As we've talked about before, many women on dysfunctional boats become passengers. Without the distraction of navigating, or sail handling, etc., her consciousness becomes more involved in this seemingly disconcerting motion and corresponding seasickness.

When Megan and I first left the Golden Gate to shake down our Peterson 46 in the open ocean, I was watching very closely for those initial signs of seasickness. Sure enough, as we moved out into the six foot swell for the first time (a pretty mellow day) she started moving a little slowly and slightly "drunkenly." She also started to yawn frequently for no reason. I seized the opportunity and got her moving. Nothing will bring on the seasickness faster than giving in to that initial fatigue and lying down for some rest. Instead, I got her up and trimming the sheets as I adjusted course for absolutely no reason. Taking her mind off of her stomach and getting the blood flowing seem keep seasickness from setting in.

Aside from the traditional and well-documented treatment: scopolamine, ginger tablets, wrist bands, etc. (Some of which have nasty side affects such as fatigue, blurred vision, and even hallucinations, and should be limited whenever possible), giving her knowledge, experience, and something to do will do more to help with her "mal de mer."

Funk

For some reason, cruising can breed personal funk. Perhaps it's the low latitude sun, warmth, humidity and constant perspiration. Maybe it's, "rail tail" from sitting stationary for long periods while underway.   Maybe it's the awkward wiping procedure forced by a toilet area smaller than a laundry hamper. Whatever the reason, it is really easy to stink on a cruising boat.

As a man, you are probably fine with a weekly hose-down on deck. Your armpits don't really stink until mold starts growing. A little talc in the shorts and socks every morning will freshen you up. Shave? Hell no. You're a seagoing captain now. Am I right?

She however has standards and is not going to tolerate the funk: yours or hers. Aside from an unlimited supply of fresh water (which we talked about in previous chapters), there are a few must-have products to keep her feeling clean and presentable: diaper rash cream, baby wipes, and baby powder. Not only do these products contain a fragrance mixture that soothes the inner beast of any woman, but they will help to calm those common itches and smelly conditions that will make both of you very unhappy.

Sugar consumption, especially simple sugars like fructose and sucrose are the perfect nutrients for all of the bacteria that lead to body odor. Limiting sugar consumption isn't just good for the waste line and blood sugar levels, but also for skin and complexion as well.

Stress

Whether within or outside of your control, sometimes everything goes to hell in a hand basket. Your reaction to crisis will be different than your wife's, as will your responsibilities and obligations. While your primary motivation is always going to be the safety of your wife and the boat (in that order), you must also consider her feelings and emotional well-being as part of the, "welfare of the crew."

We react differently

A study at UCLA found that under stress, men's bodies react differently than women's. When stressed, men produce adrenaline, which help prepare for the fight or flight reaction. Blood pressure elevates, blood sugars are readied for use in muscles, heart rate increases as does respiration. When stressed, we men prepare for battle...or to run from it.

Women's bodies react in a completely different way when stressed. When confronted with a stressor, her body releases oxytocin, which is a hormone that triggers an urge for interpersonal interaction and closeness. When the stress level aboard is generally high, or you are dealing with a crisis of some sort, she will want to be near you, and may also want to be in the company of others.

These natural in-born reactions can lead to conflict between you and your wife in stressful situations. While you will want to aggressively tackle whatever problem you are faced with, your wife will want more than anything to talk through and vent about the problem.

Without conscious adjustment, these natural tendencies will lead to interactions where you feel stifled in your attempt to resolve the stressor, while she will feel alone and abandoned. Both cases will lead to more stress, not less. When things go to shit, stay cool and keep talking.

Moodiness

Either one of you can be more prone to moodiness aboard a boat, but she's different, no? Sometimes it seems that two or more individuals inhabit the same body. In the morning she is sweet and loving and kind, and in the afternoon nothing can forgive that awful injustice of leaving the toilet seat up.

As men, we frequently just pass this moodiness off as hormonal. *It's just that time of the month; she just gets that way sometimes; or she's just tired or stressed out.* More often than not, I have found that she is most likely riding a roller-coaster ride of blood sugar. This can be especially problematic on a boat.

Blood sugar

The issue is this: our bodies are efficient machines. We consume fuel, be it proteins, carbohydrates, fats, etc. These fuels are converted into energy through various biochemical reactions within the body. This energy can be easily burned through activity. You eat a big breakfast then head out to the garage to organize. You have lunch and go for a quick walk, or work up a sweat in your afternoon presentation. In essence, you are able to burn excess energy by doing things and your body naturally regulates your blood sugar levels.

This isn't always practical aboard a cruising boat. If you are underway, there may be nowhere to go and no way to burn the excess energy. If you are on the hook, it may not be convenient to swim to shore or go for a hike. The body is forced to produce higher levels of insulin to deal with the increased blood sugar levels. Afterward, the insulin levels are too high, and blood sugar levels drop. She becomes anxious, irritable, and dare I say "cranky."

The best solution is to cut simple sugars and simple carbohydrates out of your diet completely. Eating a higher protein diet has been shown in some studies to increase overall happiness and stabilize moods. One great side effect from a higher-protein diet is lower body fat which will make her feel good about herself.

Unhappiness

Her tolerance for discomfort will vary from yours and she may complain. She may question your decisions, or argue about the same sorts of husband-and-wife stuff that she did on shore. In a confined space, all of this is horribly amplified. Thankfully, the same tactics that work on shore work on the water.

Complaining

Some women are more prone to complaining than others. "It's too hot, too cold, too rolly, the water tastes bad, the locals aren't friendly, that other boat was gossiping about us, the wind generator is noisy, the head smells bad, the cushions are wet, etc., etc., etc." Your wife might not find fault with every little issue, but when she does inevitably complain about something, your best tactic is to just listen.

Doing and saying nothing may go against your instincts, especially if you are an attentive, caring (or guilty) husband; your intuition tells you to act, to fix, to solve and to repair. If you aren't able to change or fix whatever is bothering her, your reaction may be frustration, either with the object of her complaint or with her herself.

This obviously won't help the situation. Your best move is to sit there nodding your head in agreement. In most situations your wife just wants to be listened to and acknowledged. Venting will help her settle down and that will most likely be the end of it.

Arguing about tasks

If she argues about a task or job or role on board, give her a choice. "That's fine honey don't sand the cap-rail. Would you rather disassemble the cockpit winch and lubricate it?" Giving her a choice gives her perceived control and power over herself. She just might take you up on the offer, which is a great time to support her in taking more responsibility of technical tasks.

Neutralize arguments

Sometimes complaints escalate to arguments. These are times when she might feel manipulated or taken advantage of (this can be the case if you haven't managed her expectations or oversold *The Dream*). She might feel that you are to blame for the rolly anchorage or the foul tasting water. In this case, she is looking for a fight. There is an easy way to neutralize this assault without provoking or escalating, and without appearing weak or even apologizing:

1. Listen. "The water is so awful that I can't even make tea! I can't believe you'd drag me away from our wonderful kitchen in Seattle for THIS!" Give pause, and perhaps just wait for more to come spouting up. When she stops for breath,

2. Paraphrase back to her what she just said. "I know. The water tastes so bad that it's hard to cook with." "We never had to deal with this back home."

3. Use the same phrases and words that she does. If she says that the water is, "awful," don't try to dress it down as, "un-tasty." Say it is, "awful," just like she did.

4. Build her up and *legitimize* her complaint. "I know you're not accustomed to this water. You shouldn't have to deal with the terrible taste."

5. *Confirm* and *legitimize* her feelings. "If I were you, I would be pretty upset by this."

6. Ask her what she would like you to do about it. "Honey, what would you like for me to do about the bad water?"

7. Tell her how great she is handling all of the "hardships" and that Susie and Mary would never be as adventurous as her.

By handling her aggressive complaining or arguing this way, you have accomplished several important things. You have exhausted her reasoning and diffused her tirade: she has fully "vented." You've made her feel cared for by listening, agreeing with her, and stroking her ego. Finally, you put the ball in her court. She is left to suggest a solution.

At this point, it is really unlikely that she will say, "Let's sail the two hundred miles upwind to get back to that island that might have cleaner water," or "let's dump the tanks overboard, bleach the system, and get the watermaker running again." Rather, she'll likely end the tirade without suggesting a solution, or suggest a solution that is relatively easy to carry out like adding a little Crystal Lite to the water.

Power Struggles

Most power struggles between husband and wife happen

when one feels controlled by the other. This can happen on a boat when she feels "ordered around" by the captain (you). She reacts by questioning your actions and your judgment [excessively]. When you first suspect that a power struggle is brewing, do the following:

1. Stay calm. Don't be reactive. Your best tactic is not to respond if she starts questioning. Don't ignore her; appear intensely busy instead.

2. Speak slowly. He (or she) who controls the tempo of a conversation controls that conversation. By speaking slowly, you will force her to speak slowly, which will tend to calm her.

3. Be patient. Many emotions will pass within a minute or two if the reactive dynamics don't kick in. Her anxiety may naturally pass, along with her need to control the situation.

4. Be kind. She is questioning your authority and trying to control the situation because she is anxious and fearful. Think of her as a wounded animal. Your kindness and soft touch shouldn't be condescending, but you should try to empathize with her to help her relax.

5. Give her a task. Nothing will break a control freak's need for power like distraction. Give her something to do, even if it is not yet necessary. She will feel in control of her own destiny.

Remember that if she is being a control freak, it's not [necessarily] that she's questioning your authority, but rather that she is trying to protect herself because she feels incapable and helpless. This compulsion was probably in your relationship before you ever decided to go cruising; just remember, it's not personal.

When she's pissed at you

When her complaint is specifically about you, you'll want to take another approach. If she says angrily, "I don't like the way you are treating me," ask her to get as specific as possible. If you are confused, have her explain exactly what you did or said to offend her. Don't let her get by with, "you always," or "every time…" Instead, ask her to drill down to what you just did to set her off.

At the same time, you'll want to do everything you can to try to get her to calm down and re-establish report. You can do this by: opening your body; uncrossing your arms or legs. Match her gestures; if she is making gestures with her hand, mirror those with yours. Speak at the same rate, i.e. if she is talking quickly while you talk slowly, you will appear condescending. If she is talking slowly while you talk quickly, you will come off as aggressive and angry.

Whatever you do, don't retreat to "yes, dear." Not only will this not resolve the conflict or diffuse her complaint, it will likely inflame her more and lead to a worse argument. She will not feel listened to or cared for and will likely just save the fight for another day.

How to apologize

When she is specific about her complaint against you, it is entirely possible (even probable) that her complaint is legitimate. When it is, here is the best way to apologize.

1. Take full responsibility. Don't backtrack through the chain of causality putting blame back on her. She is angry because her ego or sense of importance has been damaged by whatever "you," did. If you try to be reasonable at this point (I did this because you did that, etc.), her ego has not been repaired, and she will remain angry.

2. Don't forget to say the words "I'm sorry." For some

reason, these words have a medicinal affect. Genetics? Secret code? I don't know, but they have to be used.

3. Show remorse. She has been diminished or lost power in whatever has happened to precipitate her anger. The only way to re-establish that perceived power is to ask, "Honey, what can I do to make it up to you?" She likely won't have an answer, and if she does it will be minor and trivial. Go with it.

4. Later, once things have cooled off, come up with a procedure, a method, a checklist, or whatever that will ensure that whatever precipitated the anger won't happen again. This may or may not be effective in reality, but it is truly the effort that counts most here.

5. When the time is right, insert a little humor. Laughter is the best medicine by physically releasing pent up stress.

Whatever you do, don't stay angry for long. All boats are small, but they get so much smaller when you aren't getting along. If you allow things to escalate too far or don't settle whatever is bothering her, the boat could get too small for the both of you.

"I Want Off"

It doesn't happen often, but with the number of solo "cruisers" you find living in foreign marinas (not really cruising), I suspect this happens a lot more frequently than you'd think. Obviously these stories don't typically get a lot of press in the cruising magazines, but maybe they should be told as a warning to the rest of us.

This endeavor is obviously a _dramatic_ shift away from life ashore. You can conceptualize it now before you go, but the experience is more emotionally rigorous. I don't want to give you the impression that cruising is a life full of stress and trauma, but it is a life full of uncertainty and facing the unknown. Embracing the unknown is part of the wonder and excitement of going, but it does take time to adapt emotionally, especially for your wife.

Call time-out

It is entirely possible, even likely that your wife may need to take a break from cruising in the first six to twelve months to decompress, re-evaluate, and get her emotional legs back under her. Sometimes a little distance and perspective will help her remember why she wanted to leave her old life to begin with. The crews we know who did step away from the boat for backpacking or other land travel came back renewed and refreshed, ready to sail on.

Plan a break

An even better idea is to plan an escape from the boat in the first year. This will give her something to look forward to. If she needs a break before the appointed time, at least you will have budgeted for the land travel, airfare, etc. from the beginning, and it won't look as though it's coming out of the *cruising kitty*.

I sure wish we had adopted this strategy for our first cruise. Instead, we let the emotional fuel tank get too low.

Swallowing the Anchor

As hurricane season approached and the weather in the Sea of Cortez went from warm and pleasant to unbelievably hot and humid, we put the boat on the hard for the hurricane season and headed back to the states. Within a month, I was back on television in Denver, and Megan was working at a hospital. Even though we had told ourselves it was just a summer stop, life ashore quickly grabbed hold and a dirty boat down in the desert didn't look so appealing anymore.

We attempted to commute to Mexico for long weekends and a miscellaneous week here and there, but most of that time was willed with boat chores and very little sailing. We sold the boat a year later at a huge loss financially but also spiritually and emotionally.

Regardless or how many highs and lows you experience while out cruising, remember that overall <u>this should be fun</u>. If you or she or both are not enjoying the experience in its totality with all factors considered, it may be time for a hiatus or even swallowing the anchor for good. Just about every couple we've met who finished with their cruise on a positive note naturally came to a point where they thought, "It is just time to be done." They left the cruising life ready to face new challenges back on land.

About half of the cruisers we've kept in touch with from that first trip say that they plan on going *out there* again some day. Like Brett Favre or Lance Armstrong, they swallow the anchor with unfinished business. Like Megan and I, they always keep an eye to the sea, knowing full well that they will be back out there some day.

11.
Start Now

The most important lessons you'll learn from making *the cruising dream* a reality have nothing to do with sail trim and navigation. Cruising will completely reorganize your values and priorities, strengthen you in ways you didn't know you were weak, and change the way you see yourself and the world around you. You are already on the journey; *The Dreaming* itself is the first step. Don't stop there.

There's absolutely no reason why you can't start preparing to go cruising today. Even if you don't have the green light from your wife quite yet, you can start on the path right now without leaving her behind. Here are a few steps you can take in your day-to-day life right away to get ready for life aboard a small boat; no boat and no permission required:

1. Simplify
2. Save
3. Get fit
4. Learn new things
5. Conquer fears
6. Be grateful

None of these ideas and practices requires a dollar be spent on boat gear, so you certainly don't need your wife's blessing. However, each is fundamental to living *The Dream*.

When you do eventually end up *out there* (and inevitably come back), you'll realize that the boat itself is not *The Dream*, but an instrument and a tool in the pursuit of *The Dream*. You'll understand that cruising isn't just a lifestyle, but an attitude. Start cultivating that attitude when you finish these last pages.

Simplify

Cruising isn't so much a minimalist lifestyle, but a simplified and distilled one. One of the most pleasurable things about living on a boat and traveling to new places is that you learn what you do and don't need in your life to live happily, and learn to appreciate everything you have. Food, water, and shelter take on a new level of primary importance when you are directly responsible for them at all times. You'll begin to see that the rest of the "stuff" in your life tends to distract and get in the way of genuine experience.

You can live a more simplified life today:

1. Sell what you don't use and don't need if they have value, and give the rest to charity. Get rid of all but the clothes you wear on a weekly basis.

2. Get rid of extraneous media. Cable news? Cable television even? Not necessary and won't be missed. Magazines and newspapers that you only skim? Cancel them. CD collection? Upload to your hard drive and sell the disks.

3. Extra vehicle? Sell it. If you can take mass transit or car-pool, give it a try for a month. Go to one shared car if you can.

4. De-clutter your home. Rent a storage locker and put half of your stuff away. Anything that you forgot you had; get rid of it.

5. Eat in. Learn to cook in if you don't already. Use raw materials instead of mixes. Learn to cook on a simple stove with one or two burners.

6. Conserve everything. Become a power-hound by ruthlessly using only the lights you need at any one time. Don't let the sink water run, and limit your shower length.

7. Clean. Keep your home picked up and clutter free.

Save

Cruising is one of the most expensive ways to travel, but also one of the least expensive ways to live. For those of us without a trust fund, we'll be relying on savings or investments to fund this dream before and during, so learning to save every dollar is paramount.

If you aren't extremely frugal already, learn to cut your budget to the bone. If you don't have a budget, make one and analyze every expenditure. Aside from the tips above, here are a few other hints on saving more money:

1. Stop shopping as recreation! Shopping has become a sport today. From now on, re-think every purchase, and only buy what is absolutely essential.

2. Buy second-hand when possible. See how little you can spend when you do need to buy something.

3. Make gifts. Gifts from the heart mean more than a sweater or gift certificate anyway.

4. Entertain in. DVDs instead of new releases at the

theater.

5. Bring your lunch to work and save $200 per month instantly.

6. Vacation close to home. Instead of Bora Bora, camp at Yosemite.

7. Budget and cut ruthlessly. Break your spending down by the day if you have to. You will be amazed at the savings you will find in every category.

8. Open a cruising kitty savings account and put all of your savings above in there and watch it grow.

Get fit

Cruising is more work that you probably expect. It isn't always particularly strenuous work, but it is physical work that often requires agility, balance, and flexibility. Aside from the normal rigors of sail handling, you'll be carrying heavy things on unstable platforms, pushing dinghies through the shore break, and bending at odd angles to reach that one screw behind that bulkhead. Physical fitness on board is really important to safety and happiness.

If you're nursing an injury, meet with a physical therapist to work out a treatment plan. If you could stand to shed a few pounds, join the gym or hit the pavement now. If you are stiff and have bad posture, get yourself to a Pilates or yoga class. Adjust your diet to trim calories, take vitamins, and do whatever is required to lower blood pressure, control cholesterol, etc.

Learn

Aside from taking the obvious sailing and cruising classes, become curious about the world around you. Learn a new language. Take an oceanography course at the university or community college. Become a history buff about the areas you'd like to cruise to. I've always found that knowing more about the history of a place gives me so much more appreciation for it once I do have the opportunity to visit.

There are all sorts of skills you can learn that are not boat-specific but will be helpful when you do eventually go. You might want to consider getting instruction in:

- Welding
- Machining & Fabrication
- Fiberglass repair
- SCUBA Diving
- Basic electrical
- Basic plumbing
- Refrigeration
- Diesel Mechanics

Conquer your fears

Inevitably, you'll be tested on the journey, and you'll have to face your fears. Cruising will push your boundaries, and you will develop new levels of self-confidence. I suspect this might be one of the subconscious reasons that you are drawn to cruising in the first place: you want to test yourself and grow. Why not start now in other parts of your life.

If you are afraid of public speaking, take a class or join a club. If you are afraid of heights, learn to fly a small plane. If you are afraid of leaving the security of your career, strike out with a side business and test the entrepreneurial waters. Whatever it is you are afraid of, face that fear head-on.

Be grateful

After you've anchored your boat off of a few isolated villages, traded pearls with a remote pearl farmer on an atoll, swapped sea stories with open boat fisherman, and dined with a copra farmer, you'll have a new appreciation for the opportunities you've had in your life and the resources you've been blessed with.

Have gratitude for everything you have in your life right now, most importantly your wife. She is the missing piece in many men's cruising dream. If she's on board, let her know how special and important her commitment to *The Dream* is to you. Even if she is not yet on board, let her know every day that she is the most important thing in your life.

A Parting Word

I've waited until the end to let the cat out of the bag: the truth is that you can't really sell your wife (or anyone for that matter) on any dream, let alone *the cruising dream*. Her dreams, like your dreams come from the inside. You can't *Get Her On Board* by manipulating, incentivizing, or tricking her, but you can appeal to her needs and motivations, many of which you share. You'll be surprised by the result.

We are all human beings first and foremost, and we all share innate needs and desires: we all want to feel free and in control of our own destinies. We all want to be a part of a community of like-minded friends and family. We all want to have realistic and attainable goals. We all want to feel as though we are learning, growing, and progressing in our lives. These are the tenets of a happy, fulfilled life, and cruising offers all of these things. By focusing on these ideas rather than boat gear or visions of crystal-clear blue water and white sand beaches, you will gain a partner in *The Dream* instead a passenger in your fantasy.

Living *The Dream* is as much an inward journey as an outward journey. The captain you become starts before you ever move an inch on the chart. Becoming that captain starts today, with how you approach your commute, your job, the grocery list, and especially your wife.

You will go through periods of doubt, but once you are *out there*, the discoveries you make on the chart will pale in comparison to those you make about yourself and your wife. You will grow in ways that you never thought possible, and your lives will be different forever.

Regardless of what boat or ocean you sail or for how long, you will return one day and meet someone on the dock with that same familiar twinkle in his eye. He may ask you about the boat or the trip or your opinion about equipment, etc. The only advice that will come to your mind will be this:

If you want to go, then go. If you are serious about this dream, don't waste another day. Go now; don't wait. Go. You won't regret going, but you will regret not going.

So my last piece of advice is this: Get Her On Board and Go.

Thank You

Thanks for purchasing my book and reading to the end! I hope that you have found it useful. This is the book that I wish I had been able to read when I first caught the cruising bug so long ago. It would have saved Megan and me a lot of time, money, and frustration.

I sincerely want to help you achieve *The Dream*. If I can be of any personal help, please feel free to email me anytime at:

nick@getheronboard.com

nick@nickokelly.com

I will make every attempt to answer your email in a timely manner. Megan and I do live our version of *The Dream*, part of which means we are out of communication for periods of a week or more. I will get back to you though.

Please also visit www.getheronboard.com to see my latest projects aimed at helping people live *The Dream*.

Appendix A

References

Aronson, E., B. Willerman, and J. Floyd (1966). The effect of a pratfall on increasing interpersonal attractiveness. *Psychometric Science*.

Csikszentmihalyi, M. (1990). *Flow*. New York: Harper Collins Publishers.

Freedman, J. L., and S. C. Fraser (1966). Compliance without pressure: The foot-in-the-door technique. The Journal of Personality and Social Psychology.

Heath, C. and D. Heath, (2007). *Made to Stick.* New York: Random House Publishing Group.

Kimura, D. (2002). Sex Differences in the Brain: Men and Women display patterns of behavioral and cognitive differences that reflect varying hormonal influences on brain development. *Scientific American*.

Leonard, B. (1998). *The Voyagers Handbook*. Camden: International Marine / Ragged Mountain Press.

Riley, W. and V. K. Chow (1992). Asset Allocation and Individual Risk Aversion. *The Financial Analysis Journal*.

Vroom, V. H. and P. W. Yetton (1973). Leadership and Decision-making. Pittsburgh: University of Pittsburgh Press.

Walster Hatfield, E. (1965). The effect of self-esteem on romantic liking. Journal of Experimental Psychology.

Zimbardo, P. and J. Boyd (2008). The Time Paradox. New York: Simon & Schuster.

Sailing Schools

Blue Water Sailing School

922 NE 20 Ave.
Ft. Lauderdale, FL 33304
800.255.1840

http://www.bwss.com

Tethys Offshore Sailing for Women

2442 NW Market St. #498
Seattle, WA 98107-4137
http://www.tethysoffshore.com/

Sea Sense Sailing and Powerboating for Women

P.O. Box 1961
St. Petersburg, FL 33731

http://www.seasenseboating.com/

Appendix B

"The Storm"

We passed uncomfortable just after sunset, quickly skipping over worrisome and right into solid, engulfing fear an hour after the last light in the western sky had faded to pitch black. By then, I was too busy keeping myself and my wife alive to worry about how much worse it could get. It did get worse. Much worse. Panic didn't cross my mind until just before midnight, which was about three hours too late.

I had done plenty of scary things in my life, but I hadn't ever panicked, and I never have since. I can tell you today that panic is without decision. Panic can't *set in* any more than a fall from a tall building can *set in*. Panic contains within it irreversibility, and a swiftness like a shot to the gut. Panic is the realization that there are no options, no alternatives, and that there simply is no decision to be made.   There is no room for interpretation, no space to create meaning: there is only doing or not doing.

Wide eyed and with a sick sense of what lay ahead I said to Megan, "you should get your harness on and clip in."

After years of proposing, convincing, bugging, and committing, Megan had decided to come along for what we planned would be a five-year cruise to the South Pacific and beyond. We had both sacrificed so much for this dream; my dream. Good careers, children, family, and security had been put on hold. Houses, furniture, and cars had been sold. Every discount had been taken, and every dollar saved. Hundreds of thousands of dollars had been spent, and we even gave away our cats. A storm at sea in international waters just four days into "The Dream," is not what I had shown my wife in the brochures.

Winds had quickly built to a sustained 50 knots with gusts to hurricane strength, pushing steeper and steeper seas across our stern quarter. With the mainsail reefed and the headsails furled, we were still surfing wave faces at 14 knots (almost twice the hull speed of the boat) surging in and out of control every ten to fifteen seconds. Each passing wave launched the boat forward like a 35,000 pound surfboard. Turbulence over the rudder rattled the control lines leading to the helm and the wheel vibrated in my hand like an unbalanced tire at freeway speeds. With any momentary lull in the sounds of the wind and waves all around, I could hear the sick wine of the propeller shaft and transmission freewheeling at twice its maximum rate, moving too fast to slam into gear as the manufacturer requires.

Emergency procedures from my flight training days popped into my head: *aviate, then navigate, then communicate*. First things first: *control the boat!*

Next: Now where are we going? Megan called our course over the ground on the cockpit computer as the boat yawed through 120 degrees, plotting our position on the notoriously inaccurate Mexican chart. "I think there is something up here...," she yelled, handing me the chart, "what is this?"

Surely there was a mistake on her plot. I checked and rechecked Megan's pencil marks against the GPS and electronic chartplotter as I continued to hand-steer (the autopilot had overheated from the extreme course corrections and quit), but her navigation was spot-on. I literally couldn't believe my eyes. My mind ran through the alternatives: there had to be another option, another route, an alternate course of action, but there wasn't. We were in true, mortal danger - not movie danger or creepy-guy on a dark street danger, but sick to your stomach, pee-your-pants, we-may-die-here danger.

The crest of every fourth or fifth wave lifted us high enough to get a quick peak of one of two off-shore buoys marking Thetis Bank, a seamount shoal that stood between us and open ocean. There was no way around: we'd be forced across this bank, or would be forced onto the rocks of Cape Lazaro itself. There was no one to call, no one to notify, no one to ask for advice, no one to check in with, and no one to help should the boat capsize. In fact we hadn't heard anything but the occasional panguero on the VHF for two days or so. There was no one out there except us. Had we tried to launch the life raft, it would have been launched downwind before it was half inflated.

"Faaaaaaaaaaaaaack," I yelled with full volume and effort, but the screeching wind stripped my frustration of expression, carrying it to the empty darkness to leeward.

Relentlessly, wave after wave swept in from the northwest: hissing, crackling, and moving ten times faster than I had ever imagined a storm-swell would. The boat lifted violently, accelerating forward then slammed down into the next wave trough with tremendous stereo sound, water washing down the sidedecks with enough force to sweep you off your feet. I would have cried if there were enough time to allow the emotion, but the next wave bearing down on us looked even more dangerous…and as the moon peeked over the eastern horizon and the distant outline of the Baja Peninsula, the light spilled onto the wave following. It was even bigger.

We were sailing right into the worst of it and had absolutely no choice in doing so. As we moved toward the shallower water of Thetis Bank, the sea grew more confused and chaotic by the minute. "Rogue" waves (some breaking, and some 35 or more feet tall) leapt skyward with increasing frequency, often appearing only a boat length or two away. Such waves form in the convergence of smaller waves with additive size and volume, appearing and disappearing in just a few seconds. The sheer randomness of these unpredictable monsters added to the terror as each were capable of capsizing the boat in seconds.

My mind repeatedly scanned the options: *Life raft*? It would be gone before it was fully inflated. *EPIRB (an emergency satellite beacon)*? It would be hours should someone respond in international waters. *VHF radio*? No one is listening out here, and no Mexican boat would come out into these conditions. *SSB radio*? Should have learned how to use it before we left San Diego. The inescapable truth is that should the worst happen, we'd likely die within a few minutes to an hour at most. There was no choice but to take each wave as it came. No choice.

At the helm, I was forced to handle one potential catastrophe after another, about 15 to 20 seconds apart. With practice I settled into an uneasy rhythm: laying at a more parallel angle in the trough to limit speed as the wave approached, pivoting the boat down the wave as it reared up vertically from the stern quarter so as to only expose the stern to the breaking face, then pivoting more parallel to the wave face as the boat surged forward. Still, the boat spun out of control and buried the bow time and again, and slid sideways dozens and dozens of times, with green water washing across the decks.

We were challenged further by the need to get out to open water; our course mattered. Megan acted flawlessly, calling our course over the ground and bearing to our next waypoint. Sometime in the very early morning with the half-full moon rising high overhead we crossed the Thetis Bank and headed out to open sea. Seas remained large but settled down to the 12-15 foot range. Very uncomfortable, but manageable and not life threatening.

Eighteen hours later, we were safely anchored at Bahia Santa Maria, licking our wounds. Winds continued to blow to 35 knots for the next two days. We were not happy with our choice of transportation.